The Catholic University of America
Studies in Sacred Theology
No. ~~132~~ 114

Erroneous Conscience and Obligations

A STUDY OF THE TEACHING FROM THE SUMMA
HALESIANA, SAINT BONAVENTURE,
SAINT ALBERT THE GREAT, AND
SAINT THOMAS AQUINAS

A DISSERTATION

Submitted to the Faculty of the School of Sacred Theology
of The Catholic University of America
in Partial Fulfillment of the Requirements for the Degree of
Doctor of Sacred Theology

by

The Reverend Xavier G. Colavechio, O. Praem., S. T. L.

THE CATHOLIC UNIVERSITY OF AMERICA PRESS
WASHINGTON, D. C.
1961

Erroneous Conscience and Obligations

A STUDY OF THE TEACHINGS FROM THE SUMMA
HALESIANA, SAINT BONAVENTURE,
SAINT ALBERT THE GREAT, AND
SAINT THOMAS AQUINAS

This dissertation was conducted under the direction of Reverend John C. Ford, S. J., S. T. D., as major professor, and was approved by Reverend Alfred C. Rush, C. SS. R., S. T. D., and Reverend John A. Shinners, S. T. D., as readers.

The Catholic University of America
Studies in Sacred Theology
No. ~~101~~ 114

Erroneous Conscience and Obligations

A STUDY OF THE TEACHING FROM THE SUMMA
HALESIANA, SAINT BONAVENTURE,
SAINT ALBERT THE GREAT, AND
SAINT THOMAS AQUINAS

A DISSERTATION

*Submitted to the Faculty of the School of Sacred Theology
of The Catholic University of America
in Partial Fulfillment of the Requirements for the Degree of
Doctor of Sacred Theology*

by

The Reverend Xavier G. Colavechio, O. Praem., S. T. L.

THE CATHOLIC UNIVERSITY OF AMERICA PRESS
WASHINGTON, D. C.
1961

Imprimi Protest:

> †SYLVESTER M. KILLEEN, O. PRAEM., Ph. D.
> *Abbas*

Nihil Obstat:

> REV. JOHN C. FORD, S. J., S. T. D.
> *Censor Deputatus*

Imprimatur:

> †STANISLAUS V. BONA, D. D.
> *Episcopus Sinus Viridis*

December 27, 1960

COPYRIGHT 1961
THE CATHOLIC UNIVERSITY OF AMERICA PRESS, INC.

PRINTED BY
ST. NORBERT COLLEGE PRESS,
WEST DE PERE, WISCONSIN

INTRODUCTION

In medieval literature, the concept of the moral conscience is very intimately connected with the concepts of synderesis and the natural law. Both conscience and synderesis incline to good and protest against evil: synderesis dictates good in general, while conscience is interested in particular cases. Both conscience and the natural law are interior lights which illuminate the moral order.[1]

The medieval theologians slowly developed and elaborated a theological tract on conscience, separated from the treatment of synderesis and the natural law.[2] Before the beginning of such tracts, the theologians were not ignorant of the particular questions concerned with conscience, but they connected them with the treatment of synderesis and the natural law. The theoretical problems involved in a treatment of conscience were first discussed around 1235, and to these practical considerations were added. Theologians began to write on the nature of conscience and to discuss its value as a norm of morality.[3] These tracts on conscience were usually contained in the treatment of human acts, and they established general principles, such as the definition and description of conscience, conscience as a rule of action, and the qualities required for its formation. It is only later, in the sixteenth century, when probabilism made its appearance, that other questions were added.[4]

This work is intended to be a study of the development of the tract on conscience in two important phases of the thirteenth century, the Franciscan and the Dominican Schools. Representing the Franciscan School, the *Summa Theologica* attributed to Alexander of Hales will be the first work considered. This represents the thinking of the Franciscans in the first part of the thirteenth century, since it seems to be a compilation of the thought of Alexander of Hales and other Franciscans, notably, John of Rochelle.[5] The writings of Saint

Bonaventure will be used to expose the teaching of the Franciscans in the latter part of the century. As representatives of the Dominican School, Saint Albert the Great and his pupil, Saint Thomas Aquinas, will be investigated.

Three questions will be developed from each of these sources, and a chapter will be devoted to each source. The questions to be investigated are: what is the nature of conscience; how does it oblige; does one do a good and meritorious act if he obeys his erroneous conscience? Special emphasis will be placed on the erroneous conscience, since this question is the source of most of the differences in the two Schools. It will be shown that the Franciscan teaching on the obligations of an erroneous conscience is opposed to the doctrine as proposed by the Dominicans. Whether or not an evil action done in conformity with the dictate of an erroneous conscience can be a good and meritorious action will be investigated, and an attempt will be made to show the mind of Saint Thomas on this point.

In modern manuals of moral theology, the teaching on erroneous conscience is substantially the same as that found in the writing of Saint Thomas Aquinas. An invincibly erroneous conscience, or one in which the error cannot be overcome by the use of moral diligence or through study, is *per accidens*, a subjective norm of morality. If it prescribes or forbids, one must follow its dictates. If the error however, is vincible, i. e., it can be here and now overcome, then one must seek to correct the conscience. Otherwise, by following such a conscience, one would be committing sin.[6]

A work on this topic has special relevance today. There is a "new morality" developing in recent years called situation ethics. This outgrowth of existentialism teaches that the final criterion of morality, especially in difficult cases, is a certain interior light by which the sincere person, as it were face to face with God, decides what is permitted or forbidden to him by the Will of God. It undermines the true value of conscience because it would do away with universal objective criteria, so that conscience alone would be the final criterion of morality. In the last analysis, no absolute objective norm against which the decisions of conscience could be measured is recognized in this system. Situation ethics either denies the existence of universal moral laws or at least subordinates them to personal values. Moral law would have no absolute value, since it cannot, according to this system, possibly cover every concrete situation. God gave us the moral law as a guidepost; the individual's honest judgment on his own case makes his action right or wrong. God, then, would be interested only in the right intention of the agent, not in the objective morality of an act.[7]

Against such a concept of morality, the Church has spoken out with vigor.[8] It has condemned such a morality, pointing out that the ultimate norm of conduct is the objective right order.

Conscience has its role to play in morality. It is the subjective norm which applies to a particular act the objective law of God. The objective moral norms are founded either mediately or immediately in the very nature of things. Sacred Scripture and the Church teach various commands imposed upon men, which, if not obeyed, can be the cause of exclusion from eternal life. These norms would be superfluous if the only norm necessary were that man must follow a subjectively certain conscience. Rather, man must conform his conscience to the objective norms.[9]

This has been the teaching of theologians from the time when tracts on conscience first began to appear in the thirteenth century. In this work, it will be shown that the theologians of that time were preoccupied with the problem of preserving objective morality. The Franciscans, represented by the *Summa Halesiana* and Saint Bonaventure, went so far as to deny that conscience is to be obeyed unless it is in conformity with, or at least not contrary to, the objective norm.

The Dominicans, Saint Albert and Saint Thomas, upheld the rights of objective morality and placed conscience in a perspective in which the subjective norm was subordinate to the objective, but both were recognized as playing a legitimate role. The subjective ought always to be in conformity with the objective, but when it is not, then it is a legitimate rule of conduct only because it conforms to what is honestly believed to be the objective norm.

Thus, the *via media* is once again apparent in theology. Some would teach that only the objective order of morality has validity as a norm; others would say, only the subjective. A combination of both, correctly understood, is the teaching given by the Church. This dissertation is an attempt to show the considerations which served as a beginning of the development of the tract on conscience. It is intended to point up the problems involved in the synthesis of these contrasting elements and to show the relationship which exists between the subjective and objective norms of morality according to these great theologians of the thirteenth century.

The author wishes to acknowledge his gratitude to his superior, Rt. Rev. S. M. Killeen, O. Praem., whose fatherly interest made possible this work, to Rev. John C. Ford, S. J., S.T.D., whose interest and guidance in the role of major professor made the work a reality, to Rev. Francis J. Connell, C. SS. R., S.T.D., under whose guidance the work was begun but who was prevented from playing an active role in its development by illness, to Rev. Alfred Rush, C. SS. R., S.T.D., and Rev. John Shinners, S.T.D., who served as readers, to Rev. Charles Keating, who gave generously of his time and knowledge, and to all who by their prayers and words of encouragement have put the author in their debt.

FOOTNOTES

1. See Lottin, O., O. S. B., "La valeur normative de la conscience morale," *ETL* 9 (1932) 252, 281.

2. See Lottin, O., O. S. B., "Le tutiorisme du XIIIe siècle," *RTAM* 5 (1933) 292.

3. See Lottin, "La valeur," 252-3; "Le tutiorisme," 292.

4. See Merkelbach, B. H., O. P., "Quelle place assigner au traité de la conscience?," *RSPT* 12 (1923) 170.

5. See below, p. 1 and footnote 3.

6. See Regatillo, E., S. J., Zalba, M., S. J., *Theologiae Moralis Summa* 1 (1952) 255-62; Prümmer, D., *Manuale Theologiae Moralis* 1 (1958) 200-205; Aertnys, J., C. SS. R., Damen, C., C. SS. R., *Theologia Moralis* 1 (1950) 70-72; Merkelbach, B. H., O. P., *Summa Theologiae Moralis* 2 (1949) 42-54; Peinador, A., C. M. F., *De Iudicio Conscientiae Rectae* (1941) 15-24.

7. See Ford, J., S. J., Kelly, G., S. J., *Contemporary Moral Theology* (1958) 104 ff.

8. See Instruction of Holy Office, AAS 48 (1956) 144-5.

9. See Hürth, F., S. J., Abellán, P., S. J., *De Principiis* (1948) 136-7.

TABLE OF CONTENTS

Introduction ---V

Bibliography --XIII

Chapter I: The Summa Halesiana ---------------------------------------1

Footnotes to Chapter I --16

Chapter II: Saint Bonaventure ---------------------------------------23

Footnotes to Chapter II ---39

Chapter III: Saint Albert the Great ---------------------------------45

Footnotes to Chapter III --61

Chapter IV: Saint Thomas Aquinas ------------------------------------67

Footnotes to Chapter IV --104

Conclusions --117

LIST OF ABBREVIATIONS

CSEL — Corpus Scriptorum Ecclesiasticorum Latinorum

DT — Divus Thomas

DTC — Dictionaire de théologie catholique

ETL — Ephemerides Theologicae Lovanienses

FrS — Franciscan Studies

MG — Migne, Patrologia Graeca

ML — Migne, Patrologia Latina

NRTh — Nouvelle Revue Théologique

NS — New Scholasticism

RNScP — Revue néo-scholastique de philosophie

RT — Revue Thomiste

RTAM — Recherches de théologie ancienne et médiévale

RSPT — Revue des sciences philosophiques et théologiques

SFr — Studi Francescani

BIBLIOGRAPHY

SOURCES

Alberti Magni, Beati, *Opera Omnia*, ed. Bornget, Paris, 38 vols., 1890-1899.

Alexandri Halensis, *Summa Theologica*, ed. Quaracchi, Florence, 4 vols., 1924-1948.

Aquinas, Saint Thomas, *Opera Omnia*, ed. Leon., Rome, 16 vols., 1882-1948.

------, *Opera Omnia*, ed. Vivès, Paris, 34 vols., 1871-1880.

------, *The Summa Theologica*, translated by the Fathers of the English Dominican Province, Benziger, New York, 3 vols., 1948.

Bonaventure, Saint, *Opera Omnia*, ed. Quaracchi, Florence, 10 vols., 1882-1902.

Corpus Scriptorum Ecclesiasticorum Latinorum, apud C. Geroldi filium, Vindobonae, 73 vols., 1866-1955.

Migne, J. P., *Patrologiae Cursus Completus*, Series Graeca, Paris, 166 vols., 1857-1887.

------, *Patrologiae Cursus Completus*, Series Latina, Paris, 221 vols., 1844-1882.

WORKS

Aertnys, J., Damen, C., C. SS. R., *Theologia Moralis*, 2 vols., ed. 16, Marietti, Rome, 1950.

Bertke, S., *The Possibility of Invincible Ignorance of the Natural Law*, Catholic University Press, Washington, 1941.

Bouquillon, T. J., *Theologia Moralis Fundamentalis*, 3 vols., ed. 2, Bruges, 1890.

Caponi è Porrecta, S., O. P., *Compendium Theologicae Veritatis B. Alberti Magni*, Venice, 1588.

Concina, D., O. P., *Theologia Christiana—Compendium*, 2 vols., Bononiae, 1766.

Copleston, F., S. J., *A History of Philosophy*, 3 vols., Newman Press, Westminster, Md., 1947-1953.

Doran, W. R., *De Corporis Adami Origine*, St. Mary of the Lake Seminary, Mundelein, Ill., 1936.

Flynn, V. S., *The Norm of Morality*, Catholic University Press, Washington, 1928.

Ford, J., S. J. and Kelly, G., S. J., *Contemporary Moral Theology*, Newman Press, Westminster, Md., 1958.

Fuerst, A., O. S. B., *The Omnipresence of God: 1220-1270*, Catholic University Press, Washington, 1951.

Gilson, E., *The Christian Philosophy of St. Thomas Aquinas*, Random House, New York, 1956 (appendix: I. T. Eschmann).

------, *A History of Christian Philosophy in the Middle Ages*, Random House, New York, 1955.

------, *The Philosophy of Saint Bonaventure*, Sheed and Ward, London, 1940.

Giorgianni, V., *Pensiero morale e politico di Bonaventura*, ed. L. U. P. A., Genoa, 1947 (?).

Glorieux, P., *Repertoire des Maîtres en théologie de Paris au XIIIe siècle*, 2 vols., Paris, 1933 (vols. 17-18 of *Études de philosophie médiévale*).

Gredt, J., O. S. B., *Elementa Philosophiae*, 2 vols., Herder, Fribourg in Brisgoviae, ed. 7, 1937.

Hürth, F. S. J. and Abellan, P. S. J., *De Principiis*, P. U. G., Rome, 1948.

LaCroix, C., S. J., *Theologia Moralis, 2 vols.*, Ravenna-Venice, 1756.

Lehu, L., O. P., *La raison, règle de la moralité*, Lecoffre, Paris, 1930.

Lottin, O., O. S. B., *Morale Fondamentale*, Desclée, Belgium, 1954.

------, *Psychologie et morale aux XIIe et XIIIe siècles*, 4 vols., Duculot, Belgium 1942-1954.

Majchrzak, C. J., O. F. M., *A Brief History of Bonaventurianism*, Catholic University Press, Washington, 1957.

McGlynn, J. V., S. J., *Truth*, 3 vols., Regnery, Chicago, 1953.

Meersseman, P. G., O. P., *Introductio in Opera Omnia B. Alberti Magni, O. P.*, Bayaert, Belgium, 1931.

Merkelbach, B. H., O. P., *Summa Theologiae Moralis*, 3 vols., ed. 8, Desclée, Belgium, 1949.

Mersch, E., *L'obligation morale*, Louvain, 1927.

Murphy, B. F., *The Catholic Doctrine of Conscience*, Catholic University Press, Washington, 1944.

Noble, H. D., O. P., *La conscience morale,* Lethielleux, Paris, 1923.

Peinador, A., C. M. F., *De Iudicio Conscientiae Rectae,* ed. Coculsa, Madrid, 1941.

Prümmer, D., O. P., *Manuale Theologiae Moralis,* 3 vols., ed. 13, Herder, Rome, 1958.

Regatillo, E., Zalba, M., S. J., *Theologiae Moralis Summa,* 3 vols., (B. A. C.) Matriti, 1952-1954.

Rodrigo, L., S. J., *Praelectiones Theologico-Morales Comillenses,* 4 vols., ed. Sal Terrae, Santander, 1944-1955.

Ryan, J. A., *The Norm of Morality Defined and Applied to Particular Actions,* Catholic University Press, Washington, 1944.

Sertillanges, A. D., O. P., *La philosophie morale de saint Thomas d'aquin,* Aubier (ed. Montaigne), Paris, 1946.

Veuthey, L., O. F. M., *S. Bonaventurae Philosophia Christiana,* Rome, 1943.

Walsh, W. J., *Tractatus de Actibus Humanis,* Gill and Son, Dublin, 1880.

ARTICLES

Chollet, A., "Conscience," *DTC* 3.1 (1938) 1156-1174.

Claverie, A. H., O. P., "Théologie et conscience individuelle," *RT* 40 (1935) 422-445.

Deman, T., "Probabilisme," *DTC* 13.1 (1936) 417-619.

------, "Eclairrissements sur quodlibet VIII, a. 13," *DT* 38 (1935) 42-61.

Doucet, V. O. F. M., "The History of the Problem of the Authenticity of the Summa," *FrS* 7 (1947) 274-312.

Eugene, P., C. SS. R., "Autour de s. Antonin," *RT* 40 (1935) 211-236; 629-652.

Garrigou-Lagrange, R., O. P., "Du caractère métaphysique de la théologie morale de s. Thomas," *RT* 30 (1925) 341-355.

Gorce, M., O. P., "Le problème des trois sommes," *RT* 36 (1931) 293-301.

------, La somme théologique d'Alexandre de Halès, est-elle authentique?," *NS* 5 (1931) 1-32.

Hayen, A., S. J., "La théologie aux XIIe et XIIIe siècles," *NRTh* 79 (1957) 1009-1028; 80 (1958) 111-132.

Henquinet, F., O. F. M., "Vingt-deux questions inédites d'Albert le Grand," *NS* 9 (1935) 283-328.

Lottin, O., O. S. B., "La commentaire d'Alexandre de Halès sur les Sentences," *RTAM* 14 (1947) 93-96.

------, Les éléments de la moralité des actes chez s. Thomas d'aquin," *RNScP* 24 (1922) 389-429.

------, "L'influence litteraire du chancelier Phillippe sur les théologiens préthomistes," *RTAM* 2 (1930) 311-326.

------, "La nature de la conscience morale," *ETL* 9 (1932) 252-283.

------, "La nature du péché d'ignorance," *RT* 37 (1932) 634-652; 723-738.

------, "Le problème de l'ignorance," *RTAM* 5 (1933) 345-368.

------, "Le problème de la moralité intrinsèque d'Abelard à s. Thomas d'aquin," *RT* 39.1 (1934) 477-515.

------, "Le tutiorisme du treizième siècle, *RTAM* 5 (1933) 292-301.

------, "La valeur normative de la conscience morale," *ETL* 9 (1932) 409-431.

Merkelbach, B. H., O. P., "Quelle place assigner au traité de la conscience?," *RSPT* 12 (1923) 170-183.

Noble, H. D., O. P., "Le syllogisme moral," *RSPT* 10 (1921) 56-564.

Robilliard, J. A., DeContenson, P. M., "Bulletin d'histoire des doctrines médiévales," *RSPT* 46 (1957) 116-178.

Sala, G., "Il valore obligatorio della coscienza nei primi scolastici," *SFr* (1957) 174-198.

Smeets, E., "Bonaventure," *DTC* 2.1 (1932) 962-986.

Vacant, A., "Alexandre de Halès," *DTC* 1.1 (1930) 771-785.

Walz, P. A., "Ecrits de saint Thomas," *DTC* 15.1 (1946) 637-640.

Wegemer, L., O. F. M., "St. Bonaventure, the Seraphic Doctor," *FrS* 5 (1924) ser. 1, 5-38.

CHAPTER I
THE SUMMA HALESIANA

The authorship of the work entitled *Summa Fratris Alexandri* has been the subject of debate in the last few decades. For seven centuries, the work had been almost unanimously attributed to the Franciscan master, Alexander of Hales, who died in 1245. However, through the application of modern critical apparatus to this work, it is the more commonly accepted opinion today that this *Summa* is a compilation of the teaching of the early Franciscan School.[1]

The title inscribed in the work is explained by those who have studied this problem as being due partly to reverence and partly to the fact that the work contains much from the writings and lectures of Alexander. Whether or not Alexander had a great part in the composition of the work still seems to be an unanswered question.[2] However, there does seem to be general agreement that a great portion of the *Summa*, i. e., the first three books except for the two tracts *De Corpore Humano* and *De Coniuncto*, were written before the death of Alexander, and that his writings and those of John of Rochelle, also a Franciscan, were the main sources for this portion. Parts of the first three books and the remainder of the work seem to be later additions. Because of external and internal criteria, experts now claim that Alexander, with collaborators, was responsible for the work.[3]

The work is invaluable to our study of conscience, since it was among the first to treat of the nature of conscience and to define its normative value.[4] The work is important also for the history of the tract on conscience since it

> represents a stage in the development of western philosophy, and a tendency in that development. It represents a stage, since the aristotelian philosophy as a whole is clearly known and utilised; it represents

a tendency, since the attitude adopted toward Aristotle is critical.[5]

Gilson also speaks of its importance. He writes:
Despite its composite character, it (the *Summa Halesiana*) has a unity of its own, due to the fact that its component fragments are all borrowed from Franciscan theologians belonging to the same doctrinal school. Owing to this unity of inspiration, it remarkably illustrates what may be called "the spirit of the 13th century Franciscan school of theology at the University of Paris." Even as a collective work, it has a distinct signification.[6]

Therefore, we shall use this *Summa Halesiana* as the source of the doctrine of the young Franciscan School of the thirteenth century, without determining what is to be attributed to Alexander of Hales and what is not.

Father Copleston notes that:
it is difficult to ascertain exactly what contributions to philosophy are to be ascribed to Alexander of Hales in person, since the *Summa Theologica* which passes under his name . . . comprises elements, particularly in the latter portion, taken from the writing of other thinkers, and seems to have attained its final form some ten years or more after Alexander's death.[7]

From the time of these theologians, the thirteenth century, the tract on conscience which was incorporated in the tract on human acts contained only general principles, such as the questions: what is conscience, why is it the rule of our actions, how does it bind, accuse, or excuse?[8] It was only later that other questions were added, and later still, that the treatment of conscience became a separate tract.[9]

We are concerned here then with the doctrine, found in the *Summa Halesiana*, on the definition of conscience, the obligation imposed by conscience, and, as a corollary, what was taught about the possibility of gaining merit for placing an act prescribed by an erroneous conscience.

The first point to be investigated is the nature of conscience. Today, theologians refer to conscience as an act;[10] yet authors also admit that conscience can be spoken of as a sort of habitual knowledge of moral obligations, in which sense, we use such terms as tender, scrupulous, or lax conscience.[11] In the *Summa Halesiana*, there is no question of conscience being essentially an act, but rather, the discussion is developed to determine whether it is a separate faculty or a habit. The author of this work notes that conscience may be understood in three ways:

> Sometimes it is understood as that of which we are conscious.[12] Thus, conscience is neither a habit nor a faculty, just as a knowable thing in the soul, properly speaking, is neither a habit nor a faculty, and it is taken in this way by Saint John Damascene (*MG*, 94, 1199) when he calls conscience the law of our intellect.
> At other times, conscience is understood as that by which we are conscious, and thus it is said to be a habit by which we are conscious . . .
> It is understood in a third way as that faculty which has or receives that of which we are conscious, according to which it is said that the law of our mind is written in the conscience; thus conscience is a natural faculty of the soul.[13]

Thus, according to different aspects, in the doctrine of the *Summa Halesiana*, conscience may be either that of which we are conscious, or the habit by which we are conscious, or the faculty of the soul which has or receives that of which we are conscious. Though the author does not indicate expressly which of these meanings he accepts, he does so implicitly, since in the remainder of his treatment of conscience, he refers to it only as a habit.

Dom Odon Lottin notes that in the following articles of the *Summa Halesiana*, conscience is sometimes referred to as *quaedam acceptio rationis*. Lottin comments that this cannot be principal in the mind of the author, since he supposes conscience is a habit.[14]

The author then passes to the consideration of what type of habit conscience is. He asks whether it is a natural or an acquired habit, a cognitive or a motivating habit. He concludes that it is both natural and acquired, both cognitive and motivating, under different aspects. We shall take the first of these under consideration and see how he arrives at the conclusion that the habit of conscience is both natural to man and acquired. He notes that conscience is sometimes clean and at other times unclean. These differences are contrary to each other, and are present only by acquisition, since what is naturally present would be so always and from the very beginning. Because conscience does not always have these differences present, it must be that they are acquired. He adds a further reason for claiming conscience to be acquired. One can be conscious of something about which he was not conscious before; for example, the Jews, before the Law was given, had no conscience concerning unclean things, but after the giving of the Law, they had or should have had. Thus, conscience is acquired.[15]

Then, two reasons are given which show that conscience is a natural habit. The first reason is based on St. John Damascene.[16] He wrote that conscience is the law of our intellect. Now, the law of the flesh fights against the law of the mind, and the law of the flesh is present in man from the very beginning, from his creation. So, much more, man ought to have the law of the mind as soon as he begins to exist, and this is conscience. Consequently, since the habit of conscience is present in man from his creation, it is a natural habit.

Drawing his second reason from a gloss[17] on *Romans*, 2:14, the author writes that since the Gentiles, who have no written law, have, nevertheless, the natural law by which each is conscious of what is good and what is evil, it must be conceded that this natural law is a natural habit, and since conscience is the same as this law, i.e., by conscience one is conscious of what is good and what is evil, conscience must be a natural habit.[18]

Having given these reasons for both possibilities, the author accepts them both, affirming the habit of conscience to be both natural and acquired. He draws a parallel between knowledge and conscience, when he writes:

> As knowledge is understood either as act or habit, . . . similarly conscience which in itself includes knowledge, can be understood either as an act or a habit. Whence, conscience is such a habit, from which an act can be elicited which was not elicited previously; nevertheless, it always has some act in so far as it is an act . . . Therefore, as conscience is understood to be a habit, we concede that it is a natural habit; but in so far as it is an act, it is an acquired habit . . . Consequently, of itself, it implies two things, namely knowledge (*scientia*), and thus it can be called a natural habit; or it can imply acceptance because of the "cum" and thus it can err, and can be called an acquired habit.[19]

The meaning of the above quotation is very obscure. Apparently, the author is comparing the habit of conscience with the habit of knowledge. He says that knowledge can be either actual or habitual (knowledge is understood either as act or habit). Conscience includes knowledge, and since it is similar to knowledge (conscience is such a habit), it can also be actual or habitual. Now knowledge, as a habit which is natural to man,[20] is the power (not *potestas*, but *potentia*) to know, present in man's nature from his creation. Likewise, conscience, as a natural habit, and therefore, present in man from the beginning, is the power (*potentia*) to act, so that it can elicit an act which was not elicited previously. Therefore, conscience as a habit, always has this power to act, which concept the author expresses as "some act in so far as it is a habit." This power to act, though present in conscience as a habit, is not present in so far as conscience is an act, i.e., once the act of conscience is realized, the power to act is not present since the power is realized. Consequently, as conscience is understood as a habit, it is a natural habit, i.e., the habit which has this power to act is present in man from his creation. In so far as it is an act, i.e., as it elicits something new, conscience is not natural to man, but is acquired.

What is this act which is elicited? The author writes that the habit of conscience is always in act, always stimulates in adults the free will to good or evil.[21] It should be noted that though the author writes here that conscience stimulates to good *or evil*, this should be considered as a *lapsus calami*. In another place in the same tract, he writes that conscience is a habit which inclines to motion as in the following of good or the *flight from evil*,[22] and, as will appear in the teaching on the obligations of conscience, the conscience does not influence the will to evil but away from it. So we can conclude that the act elicited by the habit of conscience is the stimulation of the will to do good and avoid evil.

The next question taken into consideration by the author is whether conscience is a cognitive or a motivating habit. His answer is the same as the one he gave to the former question: it is both, but under different aspects. Following Aristotle (*Topic.* 4, c.5), he writes that one may not place in one category things which belong under diverse headings:

> A habit may be purely a cognitive habit, as for example, the habit of the principle: 'every whole is greater than its parts'; or a habit may be purely a motivating habit, as is the habit of a virtue; there may also be a habit which is not only cognitive, but also inclines to motion, as in the pursuit of good or the

flight from evil, and conscience is such a habit . . . By reason of knowledge, conscience is a cognitive habit; by reason of that which orders to the pursuit of good and the flight from evil, it is a motivating habit.[23]

The nature of conscience, then, according to the *Summa Halesiana* can be defined as the habit present in man from his creation, which, through knowledge, inclines him to do good and flee evil. It is not the same as synderesis, which is the "*scintilla conscientiae,* which speaks out against evil and by its dictates, naturally inclines to good."[24] Synderesis cannot err, though conscience can. This is explained by the author when he states that conscience in its superior part, touches upon synderesis and participates in its infallibility, but in its inferior part, conscience is dependent upon reason, and thus, it is possible for it to err. As conscience is a natural habit, it implies knowledge, and this is present from creation, and is infallible. As it is an acquired habit, it implies the acceptance or receiving of new knowledge, and thus it can err.[25] But error is accidental to conscience: "*quod erret, hoc non est de se.*"[26]

Conscience is also distinct from the natural law. The author compares the distinction to a thing known which directs the intellectual faculty to move in so far as it has in itself the *rationem cogniti*. "As the principle is included in the knowledge of that principle, so the natural law (is included) in conscience."[27] Thus conscience is distinguished from the natural law as the habit of a science is distinguished from the principle of the science; natural law is the directive principle of conscience.[28]

After having discussed the nature of conscience, the author of the *Summa Halesiana* passes to the treatment of the obligation imposed by conscience. However, before we begin an examination of this question, it would be profitable to make the following observation.

8   *Erroneous Conscience and Obligations*

Two statements, apparently contradictory, greatly influenced the thinking of the medieval theologians regarding the obligations imposed by conscience. The first of these is found in a gloss on the *Epistle to the Romans,* 14;23, which affirms without any distinction that everything done contrary to conscience, even though good in itself, is sinful.[29] The text from Scripture reads: *All which does not proceed from faith is sinful.*[30] The gloss notes that faith here means conscience; and everything, even though good in itself, which is not from faith, that is, everything contrary to conscience, is sinful. On this text was based the idea of conscience as a subjective norm of morality. If one followed his conscience, he was considered to be acting in accord with faith, and by acting contrary to conscience, he would commit an offense, and therefore, sin.

The second text is from Saint Augustine. He defined sin as "any act or saying or desire against the eternal law."[31] This would certainly permit the conclusion that if conscience proposes an act contrary to the divine law, one would not be obliged to obey his conscience. Thus, the norm of morality is objective: that which is done contrary to divine law is wrong. This antithesis between an objective and subjective order of morality was no doubt before our theologians when they considered the question of the obligations imposed by conscience.[32]

With this antithesis before him, the author of the *Summa Halesiana* attempts a solution of the problem of the apparent contradiction. He sees the problem in this light. The norm of morality is either completely objective, or it is also partly subjective. If it is objective, then only a conscience which is in conformity to the Law of God is binding. This would seem to follow logically from Augustine's definition of sin. If, however, the norm is also subjective, then a conscience which is erroneous, one not in agreement with the eternal law, would bind its subject to follow its dictates. This would seem to follow from the Pauline text.[33]

The author gives several reasons to prove that conscience obliges. He reasons from Saint John Damascene's description of conscience as the law of our intellect,[34] saying that since law dictates what is to be done or not done, and thus binds, so also must conscience, which is a law, oblige. He draws his second reason from the *Gloss of Lombard* on the second chapter of the *Epistle to the Romans,* verse 14. The *Gloss* notes that the Gentiles have the natural law by which they understand and are conscious of what is good and what is evil. From this, the author reasons that "as knowledge binds the intellect to that which proceeds from a knowable principle, so also conscience obliges the practical intellect to that which is known by it."[36] A third reason is taken from the notion of conscience as a judge: as a judge obliges the subject of his judgment, so also conscience, which is a judge, obliges. Another reason discussed is based on Origen's comment on *Romans,* 14;23: "The Apostle binds slothful souls, that they do or say or think nothing without faith."[37] The author reasons that if faith is conscience, then nothing must be done, said, or thought, without conscience, and, therefore, the dictates of conscience oblige.[38]

Since a conscience which dictates an act contrary to the eternal law is still a conscience, a problem of conflicting norms of morality is raised. Consequently, the author follows up with a consideration of conscience, specifically as erroneous. He gives reasons indicating that an erroneous conscience obliges. His reasons for claiming an obligation is imposed by an erroneous conscience are two in number. An erroneous conscience is nevertheless a conscience, and according to the Gloss of Lombard on *Romans,* 14;23, anything done contrary to conscience is sinful.[39] It would seem to follow, then, that this would include even an act done contrary to an erroneous conscience, and therefore, an erroneous conscience would oblige. The other reason is based on 1 *Cor.,* 8;7: *But such knowledge is not in everyone. Some, still idol conscious, eat idol offerings as such, and their conscience, being weak, is defiled.*[40] With this text as a foundation, the author states that there is no defilement without sin. In the text cited, he continues, it is pointed out that it was not because the Christians ate the meat offered to idols that they sinned, but because of their erroneous consciences, which dictated as unlawful that which was in itself lawful. The conclusion, then, is that erroneous conscience is obligatory.[41]

Taking the opposite viewpoint, and thus completing the statement of the problem, two considerations are indicated which would deny that an obligation is imposed by an erroneous conscience. According to Saint Augustine, sin is defined as "any deed, saying, or desire against the eternal law."[42] Anything done contrary to an erroneous conscience is not contrary to the eternal law, and therefore, is not sinful. Thus, there would be no obligation imposed by such a conscience. Added to this is the fact that all error must be put aside. If these considerations are valid, then it is obvious that an erroneous conscience does not oblige.[43]

The author gives his solution to this problem by distinguishing acts into five groups, according to their intrinsic morality, and then posits or denies obligation according to these distinctions. In this way, he aims to save the rights of objective morality. His distinctions follow the ideas of Saint Augustine, found in the *De Mendacio*.[44]

> There are five types of works: some are good in such a way that they can be done for no evil purpose, such as to love God for His own sake and above all things; some works are evil in such a way that they can be done for no good end, as for example, to fornicate, lie, and the like; now, there are other works which are good in general, but nevertheless, these can be done for some evil purpose, such as to give alms, which can be done out of vain glory. There are other works which are evil in general, such as to go to a brothel, but this can be done for some good reason; namely to correct the prostitute. And there are some deeds which are entirely indifferent.[45]

Using these distinctions, the writer then proceeds to state his position on the obligations imposed by conscience. A conscience in conformity with the eternal law obliges, he claims, both positively and negatively: to do acts which are intrinsically good and to avoid those which are intrinsically evil. As regards acts which are good or evil in general, conscience, in so far as it is the law of our intellect, does not bind its subject, except in certain circumstances; conscience binds one to give alms when it is formed with all the right circumstances taken into consideration, or it obliges not to go to a brothel when it has considered the attendant scandal. Conscience binds one to indifferent acts.[46]

An erroneous conscience does not bind in regard to acts intrinsically good or evil; there is, however, an obligation imposed to get rid of the error, since such a conscience would be commanding one to omit an act prescribed by the eternal law or to do an act forbidden by that law. Any bond that would be imposed by such an erroneous conscience to perform or omit an act is thus removed. In regard to acts generally good or evil, and indifferent acts, the author states that "even if an erroneous conscience, in so far as it is erroneous, does not bind, it nevertheless obliges under the aspect of conscience, as long as it is not put aside; but man is principally bound to set aside the error."[47]

The obligation imposed by a true conscience is not a physical obligation, since the subject is not compelled to act or omit the act; but it is a moral obligation, because if one does not follow the dictates of such a conscience, he sins.

In regard to erroneous conscience, the author, as we have seen above, stated that it binds in certain circumstances and does not bind in others; it binds, not because of the error, but because it is a conscience. When it does not bind, it is because of the error. This is true, he recalls, concerning acts which are indifferent, including in that term acts good or evil in general, and acts indifferent in themselves. He also recalls that his statement that erroneous conscience obliges does not hold for acts intrinsically good or evil, for in these cases, conscience must not be obeyed, but set aside.⁴⁹

To clarify his statement that a true conscience obliges one to indifferent acts,⁵⁰ the author gives two objections against his position, and by answering them, gives a clearer picture of his position in this matter. He writes that conscience is the law of our intellect, and, as such, is concerned with things which should or should not be done. Therefore, conscience deals with those acts which are determinately good or determinately evil; indifferent acts, in so far as they are indifferent, are not such acts. And if one should think an indifferent act is such an act, he is in error, and error does not oblige. It would follow, then, that conscience does not oblige concerning indifferent acts, neither by themselves, nor because of an error about their morality.

The second objection is that things which are lawful to do are either expedient or not expedient. Consequently, conscience either deals only with things in so far as they are lawful or not, or deals also with things which are expedient or not. Therefore, conscience does not deal with indifferent acts.⁵¹

The author replies to these objections:
> It must be said that conscience does not bind to indifferent acts as such, but to indifferent acts under a different aspect; that is, under the aspect of definite good or definite evil . . . but, nevertheless, conscience is said to deal with indifferent acts *in genere suo* . . .
> As for the second (objection), it must be said that conscience is concerned simply about what is lawful and unlawful; or it deals with what is expedient or not in so far as such acts are lawful or unlawful *in genere suo,* for everything is in some way reduced to the law of the mind.⁵²

The author claims then that indifferent acts in general come under the dictates of conscience. They do so, not in so far as they are indifferent, that is, specifically as indifferent, but rather *in genere suo,* that is, in so far as they are deliberate human acts, which can be good or evil. It is the command of conscience which makes these acts good or evil, for if conscience commands an indifferent act or forbids it, then according to the *Summa Halesiana,* one must follow his conscience; the indifferent act become prescribed or forbidden because of conscience.

The teaching of the *Summa Halesiana* on the obligations imposed by conscience can be summed up as follows: by its command, a true conscience obliges one to do what is intrinsically good and avoid what is intrinsically evil. It does not bind one to acts good or evil in general, except in the case where the conscience is formed with all the attendant circumstances taken into consideration. As regards indifferent acts, a true conscience binds, not because the acts are indifferent, but because a command of conscience determines such an act to be good or evil, and thus what was said about good or evil acts applies. An erroneous conscience does not oblige when it commands an act which is intrinsically evil nor does it bind when it forbids and intrinsically good act, since it cannot bind contrary to the law of God. However, there is an obligation imposed to set aside this error. As long as it persists, an erroneous conscience binds one to acts good or evil in general, and to indifferent acts; but there is also an obligation to set aside such a conscience.

How is this teaching on conscience to be understood? Is conscience actually a subjective norm of morality, or does it depend on the intrinsic morality of the acts prescribed or forbidden? The *Summa Halesiana* does speak of ignorance which excuses from sin. The author writes:

> Some ignorance excuses (from sin) and some ignorance does not excuse. For there is accidental in-

vincible ignorance, into which man falls through no fault of his own or because of the weakness of his nature, and this excuses. There is also ignorance of divine or canon law, and this excuses the unlettered if it deals with certain things not essentially necessary for salvation. On the other hand, there is ignorance which does not excuse *quoad Deum,* such as supine or affected ignorance, ignorance of those things which man is held to know, and the ignorance of negligence.[53]

S. Bertke points out that according to the *Summa Halesiana,* the more one is held to know the law, the less is ignorance an excuse for transgressions, and since everyone has an obligation to know the law of nature, no one who is ignorant of it can be excused from sin which flows from that ignorance, for the natural law is written in the hearts of men.[54] The thought expressed here is carried through in the *Summa Halesiana.* Ignorance of any law, natural, human, or divine, does not excuse those for whom the law is meant; an act performed in ignorance of a law is sinful for one who is bound by that law.[55] As for ignorance of fact, the author of the *Summa Halesiana* writes:

> Ignorance of fact is twofold: it can be of those things which one ought to know, and it can be of those things which one is not bound to know. If it was necessary to know something, and the ignorance was supine, there is no excuse and (one is guilty of) a grave sin. But if (the ignorance) was of something which one should have known, and he used diligence, such a one is excused, even if not from all (fault), nevertheless from some of it . . . Ignorance of fact concerning something which one is not bound to know . . . excuses.[56]

Is the teaching of the *Summa Halesiana* on conscience to be understood in the light of this teaching on ignorance? Is the teaching on conscience consistent with this doctrine on ignorance? It will be more appropriate to answer this question after having set forth the teaching of Saint Bonaventure on conscience. He followed the teachings of his predecessors in the Franciscan Order, as will be pointed out in the next chapter. To avoid repetition, the critique of the teachings of the *Summa Halesiana* will be given together with that of Saint Bonaventure at the conclusion of the following chapter. In this manner, there will be a more complete picture of the doctrine of conscience as proposed by the Franciscan School of the thirteenth century.

Before proceeding to the treatment of St. Bonaventure's teaching on conscience, it is our intention to point out a corollary to the doctrine of the obligations imposed by erroneous conscience. This is the question of merit. If one follows his erroneous conscience and performs an evil act, is this a meritorious act? In other words, is every act done in accordance with conscience good and meritorious? The author of the *Summa Halesiana* notes that, although an affirmative reply would seem to follow from the fact that faith is the foundation of good works, and what does not proceed from faith, i.e., conscience, is sinful, nevertheless this is not the case, for not everything which proceeds from faith, i.e. conscience, is good. What is done contrary to conscience is sinful and, therefore, *demerits,* but the converse is not true. It does not suffice for good or merit to do what one believes to be good.[57] He explains this by saying that for a work to be meritorious requires grace, which comes only from God. Therefore, he continues, to act in accord with conscience does not suffice for merit, although it may suffice that the act be good.[58]

FOOTNOTES

1. See *Glossa in Quattuor Libros Sententiarum Mag. Alexandri de Hales*, (ed. Quarrachi, Florence, 1951) 5*; this work is vol. 12 of the *Bibliotheca Franciscana Scholastica*.

2. See *loc. cit.;* Doucet, V., "Prologomena," *Summa Theologica Alexandri Halensis* 4.1 (ed. Quarracchi, 1948) LXI, LXXIII.

3. See *Glossa, loc. cit.;* Doucet, *art. cit.*, LXXX, LXXXI, CCCLXVII, CCCLXIX. See also Feurst, A., O. S. B., *The Omnipresence of God: 1220-1270* (1951) 23-27; Doran, W. R., *De Corporis Adami Origine* (1936) 4-7; Meersseman, P. G., *Introductio in Opera Omia B. Alberti Magni* (1931) 112; Gorce, M., O. P., "La Somme théologique d'Alexandre de Halès, est-elle authentique?," *NS* 5 (1931) 1-32.

4. See Lottin, O., O. S. B., "Le tutiorisme du XIIIe siècle," *RTAM* 5 (1933) 292. Though here Dom Lottin does not explicitly say that the *Summa* was among the first works to treat of these subjects, he implies it when he writes: "Ce n'est pas que vers 1235 qu'ils (i. e., theologians) commencent a disserter sur la nature de la conscience et à définir la valeur normative."

5. Copleston, F., S. J., *A History of Philosophy* 2 (1953) 233.

6. Gilson, E., *History of Philosophy in the Middle Ages,* (1955) 327.

7. Copleston, *op. cit.*, 232.

8. See Merkelbach, B.H., O.P., "Quelle place assigner au traité de la conscience?," *RSPT* 12 (1923) 170.

9. *Loc. cit.*

10. See Introduction, VI.

11. See Prümmer, D., O.P., *Manuale Theologiae Moralis* (ed. 13, Herder, Rome, 1958) 1, 196; Regatillo, E. and Zalba, M., S.J., *Theologiae Moralis Summa* 1 (B.A.C., Matriti, 1952) 252, 312.

12. "that of which we are conscious": *id quod conscimus,* is difficult to translate into English. The author is analyzing the word *conscientia,* breaking it down into its components *cum* and *scientia.* Literally, this would indicate knowledge with. The fact that the author interprets the *lex intellectus* of Saint John Damascene according to this understanding of the word *conscientia* gives us an insight into his meaning of *conscire:* that which we know which is a rule for us. Gilson notes that this is called conscience because "it confers its ultimate determination, not upon the knowing faculty as such, but in so far as it is in some way united with the

faculties of will and operation." Gilson, E., *The Philosophy of Saint Bonaventure.* (Sheed and Ward, London, 1940) 418. Saint Thomas gives conscience the meaning of *quasi cum alio scientia.* The reader is asked to bear these things in mind when the English translation "to be conscious" is used for *conscire.*

13. Aliquando accipitur pro eo quod conscimus, et sic conscientia nec est habitus nec potentia, sicut nec scibile in anima proprie dicitur potentia vel habitus, et sic accipitur a Joanne Damasceno (*MG* 94. 1199) cum dicitur "conscientia est lex intellectus nostri."
    Aliquando vero accipitur pro eo quo conscii sumus, et sic dicitur habitus quo, scilicet, conscimus . . . .
    Tertio modo accipitur pro ipsa potentia habente vel recipiente illud quod conscimus, secundum quod dicitur quod lex mentis nostrae scripta est in conscientia, et sic dicitur conscientia naturalis potentia animae.—*Summa Halesiana* 2 (edition Quaracchi, Florence, 1928) n. 421, p. 496.

14. See Lottin, O., O.S.B., "La nature de la conscience morale," *ETL* 9 (1932) 259.

15. Quia conscientia aliquando est munda, aliquando immunda; sed hae differentiae contrariae non insunt ei a natura, sed potius ab acquisitione, quia quod naturaliter ei inest, semper inest et a principio; conscienta autem non semper est sub hujusmodi differentiis; ergo non videtur esse habitus naturalis, sed potius acquisitus.
    Item, modo potest quis habere conscientiam alicujus rei quam prius non habuit, sicut patet de Judaeis, qui ante dationem Legis non habebant conscientiam de immundis, sed post dationem habuerunt vel haebre debuerunt; conscientia ergo incipit esse de aliquibus de quibus ante non fuit; sed habitus naturalis semper est de iis de quibus est; ergo ut prius. — *Summa Halesiana,* n. 422, p. 497.

16. *MG* 94. 1199.

17. *ML* 191. 1345.

18. Joannes Damascenus (*MG* 94. 1199) dicit conscientiam esse legem nostri intellectus, prout legi menti repugnat lex carnis; sed lex carnis est in homine quam cito homo incipit esse; . . . Cum ergo lex carnis insit animae a sua creatione, patet quod multo magis debet habere homo legem mentis quam cito incipit esse; ergo et conscientiam, cum haec dicitur illa; sed quod inest homini a principio et est habitus, est habitus naturalis; ergo conscientia est habitus naturalis.

Item, Rom. 2,14: *Cum enim gentes, quae legem non habent, naturaliter ea quae legis sunt faciunt, eiusmodi legem non habentes, ipsi sibi sunt lex*, Glossa (*ML* 191. 1345): "Etsi gentiles non habeant legem scriptam, habent tamen legem naturalem qua quisque intelligit et sibi conscius est quid sit bonum et quid sit malum;" sed hujusmodi lex naturalis habitus est naturalis; ergo et ipsa conscientia, quia ea conscius est quid sit bonum et quid sit malum. — *Summa Halesiana, loc. cit.*

19. Sicut scientia accipitur secundum actum et secundum habitum, . . . similiter et conscientia quae in se scientiam includit, potest accipi secundum actum et secundum habitum. Unde conscientia est talis habitus a quo potest elici actus qui prius non fuit elicitus; nihilominus tamen semper habet aliquem actum secundum habitum, etsi non secundum actum . . . . Prout ergo accipitur secundum habitum, bene concedimus quod est habitus naturalis, sed prout secundum actum, acquisitus . . . . Conscientia de se dicit duo, scilicet "scientiam," et sic potest dicere habitum naturalem; vel potest dicere acceptionem ratione eius quod dicitur "cum," et sic recipit errorem, et potest dicere habitum acquisitum. — *loc. cit.*

20. See footnotes 15 and 18.

21. . . . in adultis (conscientia) semper apparet in suo actu. Semper enim stimulat liberum arbitrium ad bonum vel ad malum, licet ipsum non ducat ad consensum: hoc enim non est actus eius. — *Summa Halesiana,* n. 424, p. 499.

22. *Ibid.,* n. 423, p. 498.

23. Est habitus pure cognitivus, sicut habitus principii: "omne totum est maius sua parte;" et est habitus pure motivus, sicut est habitus virtutis; et est habius qui non solum est cognitivus, sed etiam inclinativus in motum sicut in prosecutionem (boni) aut fugam mali, et talis habitus est conscientia . . . Ratione cognitionis ordinatur sub habitu cognitivo; ratione eius quod ordinat ad prosecutionem boni et fugam mali ordinatur sub habitu motivo. — *loc. cit.*

24. *Summa Halesiana,* n. 151, p. 199. Synderesis is the knowledge of the general rules or first principles of moral obligation. It is an infallible habit. See Chollet, A., "Conscience," *DTC* 3.1 (1938) 1163.

25. Conscientia habet duo in se: unum quod est sicut supremum, et quod hoc coniungitur ipsi synderesi, et dicit habitum naturalem; et aliud quod est inferius. et sic coniungitur magis rationi, et sic dicit rationem acceptionis quae notantur in hoc quod dicitur "cum," et sic recipit errorem. *Summa Halesiana,* n. 426, p. 500. See also

footnote 18 above, and Lottin, O., O.S.B., *Psychologie et morale aux XIIe et XIIIe siècles* 2.1 (Duculot, Gembloux, 1948) 181-2.

26. *Summa Halesiana*, n. 426, p. 500.

27. Est sicut quoddam scibile quod dirigit potentiam intellectivam ad motum, prout habet in se rationem cogniti. Unde sicut in scientia principii includitur ipsum principium, sic in conscientia lex naturalis. *Summa Halesiana*, n. 425, p. 499. Thus, Alexander holds conscience to be a habit of the will. See Frins, *De Actibus Humanis*, 59.

28. See Lottin, *Psychologie et morale*, 182.

29. *ML* 191. 1519

30. Rom. 14:23: Omne autem quod non est ex fide, peccatum est.

31. Peccatum est factum vel dictum vel concupitum contra aeternam legem. — Saint Augustine, *Contra Faustum*, 22, 27 (*CSEL* 25.621).

32. See Lottin, *Psychologie et morale*, 354-5; also Rodrigo, L., S.J., *Praelectiones Theologico - Morales Comillenses* 3.1 (ed. Sal Terrae, Santander, 1954) 411.

33. *Summa Halesiana*, 3 (1930), n. 388, pp. 387-8.

34. *MG* 94. 1199.

35. *ML* 191. 1345.

36. Sicut scientia ligat ipsum intellectum ad ea quae egrediuntur a principio scibili, ita conscientia ligat intellectum practicum ad ea quae sciuntur ab ipso. *Summa Halesiana, loc. cit.*

37. Desides animas astringit Apostolus, ut nihil sine fide agant vel dicant vel cogitent. *ML* 11. 1255.

38. *Summa Halesiana, loc. cit.*

39. *ML* 191. 1519

40. Sed non in omnibus est scientia; quidam autem cum conscientia usque nunc idoli quasi idolothytum manducant, et conscientia ipsorum, cum sit infirma, polluitur.

41. *Summa Halesiana, loc. cit.*

42. See footnote 31.

43. *Summa Halesiana, loc. cit.*

44. *De Mendacio*, 17, 18 (*ML* 40.538-40).

45. Sunt quinque genera operum: quaedam ita bona quod nullo malo fine fieri possunt, ut diligere Deum propter Se et super omnia; quaedam autem ita mala ut nullo bono fine fieri possunt, ut fornicari et mentiri et hujusmodi; sunt autem alia opera quae bona sunt in genere et possunt tamen fieri malo fine, ut dare eleemosynam, quod potest fieri causa inanis gloriae; sunt alia, quae sunt mala in genere, ut ire ad lupanar, quod potest fieri bono fine, ad correctionem scilicet fornicariae; sunt autem quaedam indifferentia omnino.— *Summa Halesiana, loc. cit.*

46. Later in this chapter, the teaching about the obligation to do or omit indifferent acts will be treated more fully.

47. In aliis autem (i.e. not intrinscially good or evil) etsi conscientia erronea, in quantum erronea, non ligat, ligat tamen sub ratione conscientiae, dum non deponitur; ad hoc autem principaliter ligatur homo, ut error deponatur.—*loc. cit.*

48. *Loc cit.*

49. *Ibid.*, p. 389. It is not determined how conscience is set aside.

50. See above, p. 11 and fn. 46.

51. *Summa Halesiana,* 3, n. 390, p. 390.

52. Ad quod dicendum quod conscientia non ligat ad indifferentia prout hujusmodi, sed ad indifferentia sub ratione differenti: bonorum definite vel malorum definite . . . ; nihilominus tamen dicitur esse circa indifferentia in genere suo . . .
    Ad secundum vero dicendum quod conscientia est licitorum simpliciter et illicitorum, vel expedientium et non expedientium quae dicuntur licta vel illicita in suo genere: omnia enim aliquo modo ad legem mentis reducuntur.—*Summa Halesiana, loc. cit.*

53. Dicendum quod ignorantia quaedam excusat et quaedam non excusat. Est enim ignorantia invincibilis ex casu, in quam non incidit homo ex sua culpa, vel ex debilitate naturae, et haec excusat. Est iterum ignorantia iuris divini vel canonici, et haec excusat simplices quoad quaedam quae non sunt necessaria ad salutem essentialiter. E contrario vero est ignorantia quae non excusat quoad Deum, utpote ignorantia supina sive affectata, et ignorantia eorum ad quae tenetur homo, et ignorantia negligentiae. — *ibid.*, n. 391, pp. 390-1.

54. See Bertke, S., *The Possibility of Invincible Ignorance of the Natural Law* (Catholic University Press, Washington, 1941) 54.

55. *Summa Halesiana*, 3, n. 679, pp. 659-60.

56. Duplex est ignorantia facti: est enim eius quod oportuit scire, et est eius quod non oportuit scire. Si necesse fuit scire, et fuit ignorantia supina, non excusat et est grave peccatum. Si vero fuit eius quod oportuit scire, et adhibuit diligentiam excusatur, etsi non a toto, tamen a tanto . . . Ignorantia vero facti quod non oportuit scire . . . excusat.—*ibid.*, n. 680, pp. 660-1.

57. *Ibid.*, n. 391, pp. 390-1.

58. *Loc. cit.* See also Lottin, *Psychologie et morale* 2.1, 365.

CHAPTER II

SAINT BONAVENTURE

Chronologically, the next theologian to whom we should turn our attention is Saint Albert the Great. However, the scope of this work is not a chronological study of the question of conscience, but rather a study of the Franciscan and Dominican Schools of this time. Therefore, we shall continue our presentation of the Franciscan school by investigating the teaching of Saint Bonaventure, the *Doctor Seraphicus*, on the problems of conscience. Saint Bonaventure studied at Paris, and probably studied under Alexander of Hales for about two years.[1] It is certain, however, that he imbibed the Franciscan tradition and was determined to keep it.[2] Bonaventure was inspired more than any other theologian of his time by the writings of his Franciscan predecessors, and he no doubt had before him the *Summa Halesiana* when he wrote.[3] He was greatly influenced by Saint Augustine, whom he regarded as the first philosopher and greatest metaphysician, and through Augustine, he obtained his enthusiasm for Plato. He considered Alexander of Hales as his master and guide, building upon the foundation laid by Alexander. Alexander had used Augustine and Aristotle for his sources, and Bonaventure also used these, drawing from them to the same degree as his teacher. He preferred Augustine, while he explained and supplemented Aristotle.[4]

The influence of his predecessors can be seen in his teachings on conscience. Like the doctrine taught in the *Summa Halesiana*,[5] the Seraphic Doctor writes that conscience can be understood in three ways.

> As the word intellect is sometimes understood as the faculty of understanding, sometimes for the habit, and sometimes for the very principle understood, . . . so the word conscience is commonly taken in three

ways.... Sometimes conscience means that of which we have consciousness;[6] and thus John Damascene says conscience is the law of our intellect; for the law is that which we know through conscience. Sometimes it is taken for that by which we are conscious, namely for a habit, as knowledge is taken for the habit of the one knowing. Sometimes conscience is taken for the power which has this consciousness, as I might say, according to which it is said that the natural law is written in our consciences. But although conscience is wont to be taken in three ways, more commonly it is taken for a habit, as is the word knowledge (*scientia*) from which it is composed.[7]

As can be noted, Bonaventure gives to conscience the more common meaning of his time, that of a habit, based on the fact that the word is composed from *scientia* which is also a habit. He continues, following his Franciscan predecessors, by showing that this habit which is conscience is both a cognitive and motivating habit, but his explanation differs from that of the *Summa Halesiana*. Whereas the latter simply states that it is a habit which, by reason of knowledge, is cognitive, Bonaventure states that it is a habit of the cognitive faculty in so far as this faculty, the intellect, is practical. This is also different from the *Summa Halesiana*, where conscience is called a habit of the will. For Bonaventure, conscience does not perfect the intellect as knowledge does, but perfects it by directing it in its operation. Thus he draws the conclusion that it is in some way also motivating, in that it dictates and inclines to good. In so far as it is a cognitive habit, conscience dictates that God is to be honored, and similar principles, which are as rules of operation.[8]

Bonaventure notes that conscience can also be considered as a power of the soul, a faculty, but in this case, he limits conscience to the cognitive faculty in so far as it deals with knowing those things which have moral overtones.[9]

Giorgianni writes:

> Bonaventure makes precise, with distinctions and clarifications, that the more common sense in which conscience is understood is that which not only designates the conscient or estimative power or that which is contained in a conscious being, but rather that by which one is conscious, and in this sense it is a habit of the intellectual faculty, which is nevertheless distinguished from knowledge in this that the latter pertains to the intellect in so far as it is speculative, while conscience is the habit which perfects the intellect in so far as it is practical, that is, in as much as it operates. In this way, the intellect can be considered as a source of movement, but not in the sense that it produces it as an efficient cause, but in the sense that it dictates the action in as much as it is a habit of judgment in operations and inclines to movement.
>
> Therefore, it is not knowledge, (*scientia*), but conscience (*con-scientia*) that this habit is called, for it does not confer determination on the speculative intellect in itself, but on the speculative intellect in as much as the faculty of will and operation are added to it.
>
> Conscience pertains to the intellectual faculty in so far as this is practical. That means that if speculative knowledge renders the intellect apt for the comprehension of a determined scientific truth, conscience confers on it the capacity to enunciate the principles to which our actions must be conformed.[10]

Bonaventure also agrees with the teaching of the *Summa Halesiana* that conscience is both a natural and an acquired habit. By natural, he means, as did the author of the *Summa Halesiana*, that conscience is innate in man, present from his creation.[11]

Dom Lottin states the position of Bonaventure regarding conscience as both a natural and an acquired habit:

> The habit of knowledge is innate, first in that the light which makes us know, *naturale iudicatorium,* is innate, and secondly in that this natural light is sufficient in itself to manifest the truth of first principles. But this same habit is at the same time acquired, first in that the terms of these principles themselves, of course, are known through the senses; acquired secondly in that, for the particular conclusions deduced from the first principles, the innate light does not suffice, but requires further information.
>
> Since conscience, then, is a cognitive habit, one must conclude that it is in part innate and in part acquired. Innate in its *naturale iudicatorium,* its first source of knowledge; innate also in the very knowledge or recognition of the first principles.... But conscience will also be an acquired habit, first since the *naturale iudicatorium* cannot, by itself, lead to discovery of the conclusions deduced from the first principles of the moral order; acquired secondly, since the terms of these first principles come to us from the senses.[12]

L. Veuthey explains this same concept when he writes that conscience is innate as is the habit of the first principles of speculation. Both are directed by an innate illumination. Nevertheless, as the habit of first principles is also in some way acquired, i.e., it acquires concepts and terms, so also is the habit of first moral principles, or conscience acquired, as regards application to particular conclusions.[13]

Thus, according to Saint Bonaventure, the nature of conscience can be described as the habit of the intellect, in so far as it is practical, corresponding in the order of action to science in the order of knowledge. It enables the intellect to decide upon the principles to which our actions should be conformed. Thus, the intellect, furnished with the habit of deciding upon the principles by which action should be directed, can be considered as a source of movement, since it dictates action and inclines the will to it by prescribing its object. This is the reason the habit is called *conscience*: it confers its ultimate determination not upon the intellect as such, but in as much as it is in some way united with the faculties of will and operation.[14]

For Bonaventure, conscience embraces both first principles and particular conclusions. Where, then, would the concept of synderesis fit in? He writes that synderesis is a habit of the will, inclining it to good; it informs conscience as charity informs faith. The natural light of the reason is called conscience, when there is question of the knowledge of moral good; the natural inclination of the will is called synderesis when there is question of the orientation toward this moral good. Synderesis is a natural movement of the will, and is therefore infallible. Conscience is dependent on reason and thus can err.[15] Both synderesis and conscience are habits which have as their object the natural law, which is the sum total of moral precepts; thus the natural law is distinguished from these habits.[16]

The question of obligation and conscience is one to which Bonaventure seems to have given much thought. He must have known the teachings of Saint Albert the Great and Saint Thomas that the obligation of conscience depends on the knowledge one has; yet he held fast to the doctrine proposed by his predecessors in his Order, namely, the obligation depends on the morality of the acts prescribed.

He asks not only what obligations are imposed by conscience, but also whether conscience obliges of itself. He writes that sin is, according to Saint Augustine, anything contrary to the Law of God.[17] If this is true, writes Bonaventure, it would seem that conscience, in itself, could not oblige to anything. If conscience should dictate an act which is not required by the Divine Law, then to act contrary to this dictate would not be a sin, since it would not contravene the Law of God. Consequently, if it would not be sinful to disobey conscience in this case, it could not be said one is held to obey his conscience. It would not be conscience that binds, but the law of God.[18]

Bonaventure himself gives us the *status questionis* concerning the obligations imposed by conscience. He writes:

> The question is, then, to what does conscience oblige? Does it bind to all which it dictates? Does every type of conscience oblige? Is a man in a quandary when his conscience dictates one thing and the divine law dictates the contrary? Which is to be complied with, the dictates of conscience or the command of a superior, when they are opposed to one another?[19]

In beginning his reply, the Seraphic Doctor, influenced by the distinction of the *Summa Halesiana* of acts according to their intrinsic morality, distinguishes three types of acts which can be dictated by conscience. Conscience can dictate an act which is in accordance with the law of God (*secundum legem*), or outside the scope of the law of God (*praeter legem*), or contrary to God's law (*contra legem*). In all three cases, the conscience dictates the act by way of command or prohibition, not by way of counsel or persuasion.[20] With this distinction in mind, Bonaventure gives his opinion on the obligations imposed by conscience.

When conscience dictates anything which is according to the law of God (secundum legem), it obliges simply and universally. The reason is simple: man is bound to the same thing by the divine law, and conscience, which is in accord with the law, shows what it is. If conscience tells one to do or avoid something which is outside the scope of the law of God (*praeter legem*), then the conscience obliges as long as it persists. Thus man is bound by such a conscience to do one of two things: he must either put aside such a conscience or he is bound to fulfill its dictates, even in the case where it would command that he lift a beam from the ground as an act necessary for salvation.[21]

It is with the third category, i.e. acts which are *contra legem,* that Saint Bonaventure finds a real problem. He writes:

> In acts of the third category, conscience does not oblige so that one must do or not do, but it does oblige that it be set aside, for this reason, that, as long as it remains, it necessarily places man outside the realm of salvation, since such a conscience is erroneous with an error repugnant to the divine law. Therefore, it is necessary that it be set aside, because, whether man does what it dictates or opposes it, he sins mortally. If he does what his conscience dictates, and that is against the law of God, and if doing anything contrary to the law of God is mortal sin, then undoubtedly, he sins mortally. However, if he does the opposite of what his conscience commands, while the conscience remains, he still sins mortally, not by reason of the work which he has done, but because of the evil way in which it as done. For he does it in contempt of God, while he believes the dictate of his conscience that such a thing is displeasing to God, although it is pleasing to Him . . . . God does not only pay attention to what man does, but also with what *intention* man does it; and one who does what God commands, believing he is acting contrary to the will of God, does not act with a good *intention,* but with an evil one, and therefore, he sins mortally. Thus, it is clear that every conscience obliges one, either to do what it dictates or to set aside the conscience.[22]

The last sentence of the above passage sums up the teaching of Bonaventure on the obligations imposed by conscience. Conscience places an obligation in every case: either one must fulfill the dictates of conscience or set it aside.

Bonaventure's opinion in this matter is much the same as that of the *Summa Halesiana*. The two opinions agree that conscience obliges to intrinsically good acts, and that indifferent acts become prescribed or forbidden according to the dictate of conscience. Both hold there is no obligation to follow a conscience dictating an evil act or forbidding a good one, but that there is an obligation to set aside this erroneous conscience.

Bonaventure's terminology differs from that of the *Summa Halesiana*, but the concepts are the same. The Seraphic Doctor adds the consideration, not found in the *Summa Halesiana*, that to act contrary to an erroneous conscience dictating an intrinsically evil act is sinful, not because one does not obey his conscience, but because of the evil intention of the agent in doing subjective wrong; for he says when one acts contrary to an erroneous conscience, he sins, not because of what he does, for that is good, but because of the evil way in which it was done, i.e., because of his intention. Therefore, according to Bonaventure, an erroneous conscience dictating an act *praeter legem*, i.e., an indifferent act, obliges as long as the conscience remains, but one may set aside such a conscience. However, if the erroneous conscience dictates an act *contra legem*, i.e., an evil act, to obey the conscience would be sinful, since this is contrary to the Divine Law; to disobey is also sinful, for one would act in this case with a wrong intention; one is bound to set aside this conscience.

In another place in his *Commentary on the Sentences*, Bonaventure makes reference to his teaching on erroneous conscience. He asks whether a sinner who receives the Eucharist, always sins mortally, by so doing. He argues that a person in the state of grace who believes himself to be in the state of mortal sin, commits a sin if he receives the Holy Eucharist. But a just person is more disposed than any sinner, and therefore, the conclusion would seem logical, that a sinner receiving the Eucharist would commit a greater sin than one who only thought he was in the state of mortal sin. However, the Franciscan denies this conclusion. He states that a person in the state of grace renders himself incapable of receiving the Blessed Sacrament, not because of any fault, but because of his erroneous conscience. As long as such a conscience persists, such a person could not communicate without holding God in contempt.[23]

When discussing the vows, Bonaventure states more explicitly how a conscience can be erroneous. He writes:

> Conscience can be erroneous in two ways. First, by dictating an obligation which really does not exist, yet denying any opposite obligation. Such an error is not dangerous, and the conscience obliges. Secondly, by judging as good that which is not good, or even evil. Such a conscience places an obligation neither to the sin nor to (any) act, but rather that its dictates be set aside.[24]

Interpreting this last passage in the light of his opinion as expressed in his treatment of conscience, it means that if conscience dictates erroneously an act *praeter legem* as obligatory, the error is not dangerous to salvation, and therefore, the conscience obliges as long as it persists. But such a conscience can also be set aside. On the other hand, if such a conscience dictated an act *contra legem,* it must be set aside, for to follow it is to act contrary to the law of God, and to disobey it is to act with a wrong intention.

As the author of the *Summa Halesiana,* so also Bonaventure had in mind the text from *Romans* 14,23, when he wrote on the obligations of conscience. He reconciles his teaching with this text by noting that it is always sinful to act contrary to conscience, for in that case, one always acts in contempt of God. However, it is not always good to act in accord with conscience as, for example, when conscience dictates something contrary to God's law. In this case, the conscience must be set aside.[25]

The Seraphic Doctor also writes that conscience obliges of itself. He answers an objection, referred to above,[26] concerning this point:

> It must be said that to act contrary to God's law can be done in two ways: either truly or interpretatively, either according to the truth or according to one's belief, and both ways are mortal sins, for one contemns God in both ways. Although acting contrary to conscience is not always acting contrary to the law of God according to the truth, nevertheless, it is contrary to his law either according to the truth or according to one's belief. The reason is that conscience is like a herald and a messenger of God, and what it says, it does not say of itself, but rather, it commands as if it were from God, just as a herald who announces an edict of the king. And thus it is that conscience has the power of obliging in those things, which, in some way, can be done licitly.[27]

Here, Bonaventure is making more explicit his teaching on the obligations imposed by conscience. He writes that one can act contrary to his conscience in one of two ways, either objectively or subjectively. He likens conscience to a herald of God, which speaks with God's authority. If this herald speaks the truth, and one does not follow its dictates, that person acts contrary to the Law of God "according to the truth," i.e., objectively. If the herald does not speak the truth and one does not follow its dictates, he acts contrary to the Law of God "according to one's belief," i.e., subjectively. In keeping with his opinion on the obligations imposed by conscience, Bonaventure states that conscience itself has the power of binding its subject "in those things which, in some way, can be done licitly," i.e., in regard to acts which are *praeter legem*, but not in regard to acts which are *contra legem*.[28] Conscience can bind us, for it is in some way superior to us, as the intermediary between God and us, as the herald is the intermediary between a king and his people.[29]

Having treated fully the question of conscience and its obligations, Bonaventure returns to his summary of the problem and finds he has still to answer two questions: is a man in a quandary when conscience and the divine law dictate contraries; and which is to be obeyed, the precept of a superior or conscience, when they conflict? He answers:

> No one is in a quandary in his conscience, except for a time; namely, as long as conscience remains. Nevertheless, he is not simply in a quandary, since man must set aside such a conscience. If he does not know how to judge it by himself, because he does not know the law of God, he should consult those wiser than himself, or turn himself to God in prayer if human counsel is lacking. Other wise, if he is negligent, that which the Apostle says is verified in him: *if anyone ignores this, he shall be ignored* (1Cor., 14;38). It is also clear that the command of a superior is to be preferred over conscience, especially when the superior commands what he can and should command.[30]

The Quaracchi editors of this work of Bonaventure have added a scholion, explaining that, in their estimation, the last sentence of this passage evinces the same teaching as that of St. Thomas in this matter. They write that the words "the command of a superior is to be preferred over conscience" must be understood with the restriction insinuated in the rest of the sentence: "especially when the superior commands what he can and should command." The superior's command would also take precedence when the subject's conscience is in doubt. The editors refer to another statement of Bonaventure to back up their contention that the rule in question is not a general one, but rather, restricted. The Seraphic Doctor writes that one is held to obey his superiors only to the extent that he promised God to observe, and in those things which are not contrary to the spirit and the rule. If a superior should command his subject to do something beyond the scope of the vow (*supra votum*), the subject would not be held to fulfill that command.[31] For this reason, the editors write that "the saying of Saint Thomas: 'the dictate of conscience obliges more than the precept of a superior' differs only in word and *in speciem* from that which the Seraphic Doctor teaches here."[32] Whether or not this is the case will more easily be seen after we have discussed the position of Saint Thomas later in this work.

We have seen above the teaching of Saint Bonaventure on the question of conscience and its obligations. At this point, it will be helpful to give a summary of this doctrine, in order that we may have a clearer picture of the opinions of the Seraphic Doctor.

All acts dictated by conscience can be classified thus: they are either *secundum, praeter,* or *contra legem Dei.* If conscience dictates an act *secundum legem,* the conscience is a true conscience, and it is evident that the act dictated is a good act. The conscience, in all such cases, obliges, since it shows what the law of God is. Should conscience dictate an act which is *praeter legem,* there is an obligation to fulfill this precept, as long as such a conscience persists in its command.

A conscience which commands under precept or prohibition, an act *praeter legem,* is an erroneous conscience; nevertheless since the error is of the type not dangerous to salvation, one may fulfill the precept, in fact, he must do so, as long as the conscience continues to command. But such an obligation is not perpetual; a little thought might show no obligation, since

God's law contains no such matter. Once a man knows he is
not obliged, there is no obligation. Thus, since such an act is
indifferent, one can also set aside the command of conscience.

When conscience dictates an act which is *contra legem*, that
is, an evil act, there is an obligation imposed to set aside the
dictates of the conscience. As long as conscience continues to
command an evil act, a man is placed in the peculiar situation
of sinning whether he obeys or disobeys; he sins by obeying
his conscience, since he acts contrary to God's law; and he
sins by disobeying the same conscience, for though the act he
does contrary to conscience is a good act, he believes the act to
be evil, and thus acts with a wrong intention. Therefore, he
is obliged to set aside the conscience.

The same question may be asked here as was asked in the
case of the *Summa Halesiana*: is this teaching on conscience
to be understood by itself, or does the teaching of Bonaventure on ignorance have to be considered, for Bonaventure
does write that all ignorance excuses from sin in some way,
because it lessens the *rationem voluntarii*. He writes that the
voluntarium includes in itself knowledge, and therefore, what
deprives one of knowledge also deprives him of the *rationem
voluntarii*.[33]

Speaking of invincible ignorance, the Seraphic Doctor
writes that if one does not know the law through no fault of
his own, as for example, a child or an insane person, he is
excused from sin *a toto*. If this type of ignorance does not
take away the full use of reason, as in one who is angry, it
excuses *non a toto, sed a tanto*.[34] Thus one would be guilty
of sin to the degree that he is blameworthy for his ignorance
and to the extent that the ignorance took away the *rationem
voluntarii*. Ignorance of the law excuses only if it does not
proceed from previous sin. According to Bonaventure, ignorance of the law is sinful if it deals with truths necessary
for salvation or for the moral life, and one can know them.

If, however, the ignorance deals with a truth of no great importance in the moral order, it may be inculpable.[35]

Now that we have seen the doctrine of both these Franciscan theologians of the thirteenth century, as representatives of that school, it will be possible to answer the question of the relationship between their teachings on conscience and ignorance, and to give a critique of their doctrine on conscience.

Both in the *Summa Halesiana* and the writings of Bonaventure, ignorance of the law in general does not constitute an excuse from sin. Bonaventure does state that ignorance of the law excuses, but only if it deals with a truth of no great importance of the moral order. This perhaps will explain his statement that a conscience dictating an act *praeter legem* is not dangerous to salvation and, therefore may be followed. But an act *contra legem* is dangerous to salvation; it is of importance in the moral order and so it would be no excuse for one to claim ignorance in this case. Both works claims ignorance of the natural law does not excuse. They hold to the profound conviction, common to many theologians of the Middle Ages, that the moral law is written in the hearts of men; that fundamental truths are inserted into man's nature, and consequently, ignorance of this seemed to them voluntary. They did not distinguish, as is done today, between the primary and the more remote conclusions of the Law.[36] So, in this manner, we can say their doctrines on conscience and ignorance are consistent with each other. The important thing here is that their teaching on ignorance does not change in any way what they taught on conscience. The criterion they used to determine whether or not conscience obliges was not knowledge, but the intrinsic morality of the act prescribed or forbidden.

From an objective viewpoint, it is true that a true conscience must be followed, that an erroneous conscience should be corrected or set aside, and if the teachings of these theologians were understood in the objective order, they would be tenable. But conscience is not an objective norm, it is subjective. The Franciscans taught that conscience was a habit inclining one to good and away from evil, but whether or not this habit was truly fulfilling its function could only be determined by having recourse to the Law. Man would have to compare the dictates of conscience with the Law of God, but then of what use would conscience be? Before one could act, he would have to determine the objective morality of the act dictated by conscience. The Franciscan tradition followed by these men underlined the needs of objective morality, to save it from being violated.[37] The whole role of conscience is reduced to being in conformity with the law. For them, conscience derived its obligatory value from the obligations imposed by Law; conscience is considered a servant of the Law, without antonomy or proper rights. It was not considered apart from the Law.[38]

These theologians posited obligations based on the objective morality of acts, not on the knowledge of that morality. Yet, Saint Bonaventure wrote that conscience is a herald or messenger from God, informing men of the Law. If this is true, and it is, as we shall see later in this work, then it is logical that man should follow its dictates. A subject must follow the edict of a king, given by a messenger, unless he has very good reasons for believing the messenger to be a false one. If he believes the messenger to be false he makes prudent inquiries to substantiate or repudiate his belief. But if he has no suspicion the messenger is false, or if he cannot substantiate his suspicion when he has one, then a subject must obey the command of the messenger. Since conscience is a messenger from God, the same holds true for its commands. It is not what the conscience commands, but whether or not man believes the conscience to be a true herald. It is hard for us to see, then, how Saint Bonaventure was logical in calling conscience a herald of God, and then basing obligations imposed by conscience on whether the message it carried was true or false. But to the Seraphic Doctor, as to many others of his time, the important thing was to save the rights of objective morality.[39] This was his goal, and the solution he offered was, in his mind, one which led to the attainment of that goal.

Bonaventure does not explicitly take under consideration the question of merit and erroneous conscience. Dom Lottin notes that up to the time of Bonaventure, there was confusion, in regard to this question, between the moral goodness of an act and its meritorious character. Before Bonaventure, theologians were content to note that man was sufficient to himself for sin, but that God's grace was needed for merit. Lottin continues that Saint Bonaventure treated the question as did his predecessors, but with this change: he did not refer to grace, thus eliminating the question of merit, and speaking only of moral goodness; Bonaventure simply stated that the objective malice of acts was opposed to acts being morally good.[40]

The Seraphic Doctor wrote that moral goodness depends above all on the right intention of the agent, but the nature of the work must also be taken into consideration. He wrote that anything which is evil in itself could not become good because of a right intention.[41] Thus, logically, it can be concluded that if an erroneous conscience prescribed an act, wrong in itself, and one performed this act with a right intention, this act would not be a morally good act, and *a fortiori*, would not be meritorious.

FOOTNOTES

1. Ce qui est certain, c'est que Bonaventure vient bientôt à Paris ou il a eu l'avantage d'être assez longtemps le disciple d'Alexandre de Halès, qu'il appellait plus tard son père et maître.—Smeets, E., "Bonaventure," *DTC* 2.1 (1932) 963.

2. See Fuerst, *The Omnipresence of God*, 22; Copleston, *A History of Philosophy* 2, 240; Glorieux, *Repertoire des maîtres*, n. 305

3. Vacant, A., "Alexandre de Halès," *DTC* 1.1 (1930) 783.

4. See Wegemer, L., O.F.M., "Saint Bonaventure, the Seraphic Doctor," *FrS* 5 (1924) 10; also Majchruzak, C., O.F.M., *A Brief History of Bonaventurianism* (Catholic U. Press, Washington, 1957) 2-6.

5. See above, p. 3.

6. *Pro ipso conscito:* see chapter 1, footnote 12, where the Bonaventurian idea of *conscientia* is thus expressed by Gilson: "it (conscience) confers its ultimate determination not upon the knowing faculty as such but in so far as it is in some way united to the faculties of will and operation."

7. Sicut nomen intellectus aliquando accipitur pro potentia intelligendi, aliquando pro habitus, aliquando pro ipso principio intellectu, . . . sic nomen conscientiae tripliciter consuevit accipi . . . . Aliquando enim accipitur conscientia pro ipso conscito; et sic dicit Joannes Damascenus, quod conscientia est lex intellectus nostri; lex enim est illud quod per conscientiam novimus. Aliquando vero accipitur conscientia pro eo quo conscii sumus, scilicet, pro habitu, sicut scientia accipitur pro habitu, scilicet cognoscentis. Aliquando autem accipitur conscientia pro ipso potentia consciente, ut ita dicam, secundum quod dicitur quod lex naturalis scripta est in conscientiis nostris *(Rom.*2,14.). Cum igitur tribus modis accipi soleat conscientiae nomen, usitatori tamen modo nomen conscientiae pro habitu accipitur, sicut et nomen scientiae, a quo componitur. — Saint Bonaventure, *In II Sent.*, d. 39, a. 1 (ed. Quaracchi, Florence, 2, 1885), 899.

8. *Loc cit.*

9. *Ibid.,* 902.

10. Bonaventura precisa, in sede di distinzione e di chiarificazione, che il senso più commune in cui si parla di coscienza è quello che non tanto designa la potenza cosciente o estimativa o ciò che si contiene in essa coscienza, quanto invece ciò per cui si è consci; e in tal

senso è abito della potenza intelletiva, che tuttavia si distingue da quell'altro che è la scienza, per fatto che questa appartiene all'intelletto in quanto speculativo, la coscienza invece è abito che perfeziona il nostro intelletto, in quanto intelletto pratico, in quanto cioè ci indirizza nelle opere. In tal modo l'intelletto può essere considerato come fonte di movimento, non nel senso però che lo produca come causa efficiente, ma nel senso che essa detta l'azione in quanto abito di giudizio nel'operare e inclina al movimento.

Non scienza, dunque, ma coscienza, si chiamerà questo abito, dal momento ch'esso non conferisce determinazione all'intelletto speculativo preso in se, ma all'intelletto speculativo in quanto ad esso si coniunge la facoltà di volere e di operare.

La coscienza pertiene alla potenza intelletiva in quanto pratico. Ciò vuol dire che, se la scienza speculativa rende l'intelletto atto alla comprensione di determinate verità scientifiche, la coscienza gli conferisce la capacita di enunciare i principi ai quali debbono confromarsi le nostre azioni.—Giorgianni, V., *Pensiero morale e politico di Bonaventura* (Edizioni L.U.P.A., Genoa, 1947 (?) 59-60.

11. See chapter 1, pp. 5-6.

12. L'habitus de la science est inné, d'abord en ce que la lumière qui nous fait connaître, *naturale iudicatorium,* est inée, inée ensuite en ce que cette lumière naturelle se suffit à elle-même pour manifester la vérité des premiers principes. Mais ce même habitus est en même temps acquis, d'abord en ce que les termes de ces principes eux-mêmes, on l'a rappelé à l'instant, sont connus par les sens; acquis encore in ce que, pour les conclusions particulières deduites des premiers principes, la lumière innée ne suffit point, mais requiert une information ultérieure.

Pius donc que la conscience est un habitus cognitif, on devra conclure que la conscience est en partie innée, et en partie acquise. Innée dans son *naturale iudicatorium,* sa première source de connaissance; innée aussi dans la connaissance même des premiers principes . . . . Mais la conscience sera aussi un habitus acquis, d'abord en ce que le *naturale iudicatorium,* ne peut, à lui seul, faire découvrir les conclusions déduites des premiers principes de l'ordre moral; acquis encore en ce que les termes de ces premiers principes nous viennent des sens.—Lottin, "La nature de la conscience morale," 277-8.

13. See Veuthey, L., *Sancti Bonaventurae Philosophia Christiana* (Rome, 1943) 236.

14. See Gilson, E., *The Philosophy of Saint Bonaventure* (Sheed and Ward, London, 1940) 418.

15. Saint Bonaventure, *loc. cit.*, a.2, qq. 1-3, 911-13. See Lottin, *Psychologie et morale*, 207, 209. This opinion on the possibility of error does not differ from that taught in the *Summa Halesiana*. There, it was written that conscience, in its superior part, participates in the infallibility of synderesis; and in its inferior part, it touches the reason, and is fallible. Thus, in so far as it is natural, conscience does not err; it errs only in so far as it is acquired. It is this which Bonaventure is here teaching. See Giorgianni, *op. cit.*, 61.

16. Saint Bonaventure, *loc. cit.*

17. Saint Augustine, *Contra Faustum*, 22,27 (*CSEL* 25.621).

18. Saint Bonaventure, *loc. cit.*, a.1, q.3, 906.

19. Est igitur questio, ad quid conscientia liget: utrum liget ad omne quod dictat; et utrum omnis conscientia liget; et utrum homo sit perplexus, quando conscientia dictat unum et lex divina dictat contrarium; et cui magis sit obtemperandum, utrum dictamini conscientiae an praecepto praelati, cum obviant sibi ad invicem.—*loc. cit.*

20. *Loc. cit.*

21. *Loc. cit.*

22. In tertiis vero, conscientia non ligat ad faciendum vel non faciendum, sed ligat ad se deponendum, pro eo quod cum talis conscientia sit erronea errore repugnante legi divinae, necessario, quamdiu manet, ponit hominem extra statum salutis; et ideo necesse est ipsam deponere quia sive homo facit quod dicit, sive eius oppositum, mortaliter peccat. Si enim faciat quod conscientia dictat et illud est contra legem Dei, et facere contra legem Dei sit mortale peccatum; absque dubio mortaliter peccat. Si vero facit oppositum eius quod conscientia dictat, ipsa manente, adhuc peccat mortaliter, non ratione operis quod facit, sed quia malo modo facit. Facit enim in contemptum Dei dum credit, dictante sibi conscientia, hoc Deo displicere, quamvis Deo placeat . . . . Non tantum attendit Deus quid homo faciat sed quo animo faciat; et iste qui facit quod Deus jubet, credens facere contra ipsius Dei voluntatem, non facit bono animo, sed malo; et ideo peccat mortaliter.—Sic igitur patet quod omnis conscientia ligat ad faciendum quod dictat aut ligat ad se deponendum.—*ibid.*, 906-7. See below, no. 30, for how conscience is to be set aside.

23. Saint Bonaventure, *In IV Sent.*, d. 9, a.2, q.3, ad 7; (ed. Quarrachi, 4,188-9) 210-11.

24. Conscientia dicitur erronea dupliciter: aut quia credit se teneri ad id ad quod non tenetur, tamen non tenetur ad eius oppositum; et talis error non est periculosus, et talis ligat. Est et alia erronea, quae credit bonum quod non est bonum, immo malum; et talis ligat non ad peccatum nec ad factum, sed ad se deponendum.— *loc. cit.*, d.38, a.1, q.2; 817-8.

25. Bonaventure, *In II Sent.*, *loc. cit.*, 907.

26. See above, p. 28.

27. Dicendum quod facere contra legem Dei hoc potest esse dupliciter: vel vere vel interpretative, sive secundum veritatem sive secundum reputationem; et utroque modo est peccatum mortale; utroque enim modo contemnitur Deus. Et quamvis faciens contra conscientiam non faciat semper contra legem Dei secundum veritatem, facit tamen vel secundum veritatem vel secundum reputationem; quia conscientia est sicut praeco Dei et nuntius, et quod dicit non mandat ex se, sed mandat quasi ex Deo, sicut praeco, cum divulgat edictum regis. Et hinc est quod conscientia habet virtutem ligandi in his quae possunt aliquo modo bene fieri.—St. Bonaventure, *loc. cit.*

28. This is the conclusion reached by Deman: L'école franciscaine a pensé que l'erreur relative aux actes bons ou mauvais spécifquement n'importe aucune obligation. . . . Le jugement de la conscience ne fonde de lui-même une obligation qu'à l'endroit des actes de leur nature indifferents. (The Franciscan school thought that error in regard to acts intrinsically good or evil did not impose any obligation. . . . The judgment of conscience only founded an obligation in regard to acts of their nature indifferent.)—Deman, Th., "Probabalisme," *DTC* 13.1 (1936) 418.9.

29. Saint Bonaventure, *loc cit.*

30. Nemo ex conscientia perplexus est nisi ad tempus, videlicet, quamdiu conscientia manet; non tamen est perplexus simpliciter, pro eo quod nescit legem Dei, debet sapientiores consulere, vel per orationem se ad Deum convertere, si humanum consilium deest. Alioquin si negligens est, vertificatur in eo quod dicit Apostolus (1 *Cor*.14;38): Qui ignorat ignorabitur.—Patet etiam, quod plus standum est praecepto praelati quam conscientiae, maxime quando praelatus praecipit quod potest et debet praecipere.—*loc cit.*

31. *Ibid.*, d. 44, a.3, q.2, 1013.

32. Dictum S. Thomae "Dictamen conscientiae plus obligat quam praeceptum praelati" (*In II Sent.*, d.39, q.3, a.3, ad3) non nisi verbo et in speciem recedit ab iis quae Seraphicus hic docet.—*Lib. Sent. Bonaventurae*, 2, 908, Scholion.

33. Omnis ignorantia aliquo modo excusat peccatum. Et ratio hujus est quia minuit de ratione voluntarii, minuit etiam de ratione contemptus. Ceteris enim paribus, magis contemnit qui peccat ex industrio, quam qui ignoranter peccat. Et iterum cum voluntarium includit in se cognitionem, quod privat cognitionem, privat de ratione voluntarii. Quia ergo peccatum mensuratur secundum quantitatem libidinis et contemptus, et ignorantia diminuit de ratione horum, generaliter verum est quod omnis ignorantia in quantum hujusmodi, excusat peccatum.—*In II Sent.*, d. 27, a.2, q.3; 2, 526.

34. *Ibid.*, 527.

35. See Bertke, *The Possibility of Invincible Ignorance*, 56.

36. See Deman, *art. cit.*, 418-20.

37. See Lottin, O., O.S.B., "La valeur normative de la conscience morale," *ETL* 9 (1932) 418-19.

38. See Deman, *loc. cit.*

39. See Lottin, "La valeur normative," 418-19.

40. *Ibid.*, 431, footnote 30.

41. Saint Bonaventure, *op. cit.*, d. 40, a.1, q.1; 2, 921; also Veuthey, *op. cit.*, 224.

CHAPTER III

SAINT ALBERT THE GREAT

The Dominican, Saint Albert the Great, did not write very extensively on the subject of conscience and its obligations, but what he did write represents a transition from the opinions of the Franciscan school to the doctrine as exposed by Saint Thomas. He wrote on th seubject in two of his many works, in the *Summa de Creaturis* and in the *Summa Theologica*. In the former, which was the first of the two,[1] Saint Albert departs from the traditional Franciscan teaching on conscience by calling it an act rather than a habit. In his later work,[2] the Dominican refers to conscience as a habitual faculty, and thus seems to return to the Franciscan concept. However, as this chapter is developed, it will be seen that he did not contradict himself nor change his tenets on this point. In this matter in general, Gilson has this to say:

> When a writing career extends over such a long time, an evolution is always possible, or probable, but only detailed research work can establish that it took place. In the present state of our knowledge, there is no reason to think that the general doctrine taught by Albert in his early *Summa de Creaturis* differs on any important point from his late doctrinal positions as we find them defined in his unfinished *Summa Theologica*.[3]

We shall investigate in this chapter in chronological order the writings of Saint Albert, taking first the *Summa de Creaturis* and then the *Summa Theologica*. The *Summa de Creaturis* is actually two tracts intimately connected; the first is the *De Quattuor Coaequaevis,* and the other is the *De Homine*.[4] It is in the latter that Albert treats conscience, but only briefly. In answer to the question what conscience is, Saint Albert replies that it is the conclusion of the practical reason from two premises, the conclusion of a syllogism.

The major premise of the syllogism is supplied by synderesis, which the Dominican defines as the habit which inclines to good through universal *rationes* of good.[5] Reason, which has the function of comparing the particular to the universal, supplies the minor premise of the syllogism. The conclusion of the practical reason from these two premises is the act of conscience.[6]

To illustrate his point and clarify it, Saint Albert gives this example: all good is to be done; this act is good; this act is to be done. The major of the syllogism, he explains, does not descend to any particular, nor does it consider whether or not the act in question is this one or that, meritorious or not, but it considers only the universal. The minor premise does not concern itself with any obligation (*non est de faciendo*), but with the reason why the act should be performed or omitted; the minor does not command that the act be done. The conclusion, which is conscience, states whether or not the act should be done or avoided.[7] Consequently, conscience may be defined as an act of the practical reason, which dictates whether or not a proposed action should be performed or omitted. It is a definitive sentence, carrying with it the obligation that it be heeded.[8]

Saint Albert then proceeds to demonstrate that this obligation is present in conscience, and he also points out under what circumstances conscience places the obligation. He argues first from authority, quoting the text, "he who acts contrary to conscience lays a foundation for hell."[9] The obvious conclusion is that conscience must impose an obligation, for to disobey it is to place one's salvation in danger. The second argument used by Albert proves that an erroneous conscience obliges, and, *a fortiori*, also a true one. He writes:

If conscience were to dictate that some act must be done by way of a precept, which (act) however is not a precept, and if one does not perform the act, he spurns, as much as he can, both the prescribing agent and the thing prescribed. Now, anyone who spurns a precept sins mortally. Therefore, (in this case) one sins mortally, and thus is obliged to perform what is prescribed, precisely because conscience prescribed it. Therefore, conscience obliges that its precepts be fulfilled.[10]

Albert teaches, then, that conscience places an obligation that its dictates be fulfilled, for by disobeying a command of conscience, man would be holding in contempt a command pertaining to the moral order, and consequently, he would sin mortally.

The Dominican then proceeds to clarify his teaching that one who would hold in contempt the dictates of an erroneous conscience would be guilty of mortal sin. He does this by raising two objections against this position and then answering them. To the objection that whatever is in error does not impose an obligation in so far as it is in error, Saint Albert replies that error, as error, does not oblige as long as it is supposed that there is an error. However, if one does not know the error is present, then the conscience obliges, since one believes it to be true. He also takes this occasion to indicate how a conscience can be erroneous. The minor of the syllogism which results in the dictate of conscience, is taken from reason, and it is this premise which can cause error to be present in conscience. If this premise were examined, and the falsity of it were discovered, then the syllogism would be invalid, and the dictate of conscience would cease. By examining the minor premise, therefore, one can correct a conscience which is known or suspected to be erroneous, and one will not be in the quandary of being obliged to do something wrong by conscience or of sinning by disobeying conscience.[11]

A further clarification of the Saint's doctrine results from the explanation he gives in reply to this objection: what is false cannot be known and therefore, cannot be in one's conscience; what is not in one's conscience cannot place any obligation; consequently, erroneous conscience cannot oblige. Albert answers the objection by stating that if knowledge is understood in the strict sense, it is true that what is false cannot be known. Nevertheless, one often imagines to be true what is false, and thus supposes he has the truth.[12]

Taking all the foregoing together, we can sum up the doctrine taught by Saint Albert the Great in his *Summa de Creaturis*. Conscience is an act, which is the conclusion of a syllogism. The major premise is supplied by synderesis; the minor, by reason. Conscience places an obligation that its dictates be followed, for by disobeying, man sins mortally, since he spurns a grave precept. Albert does not draw any distinction between a true and an erroneous conscience with regard to obligation. As long as man is convinced that his conscience is true, he must follow it.

Saint Albert, however, does not teach that man must *always* follow *any* dictate of conscience, but rather that one must be subjectively convinced that his conscience is true. The Dominican had previously distinguished various states of mind: doubt, ambiguity, opinion, and knowledge.[13] Basing himself on these distinctions, Saint Albert writes that conscience does not oblige unless the minor of the syllogism is held to be true, either as an opinion, a belief, or as something known. If the minor premise is held to be true, then conscience obliges, whether the conscience be true or erroneous. The author refers back to what he had previously written about the spurning of a precept to prove his point.[14] Thus, as long as one adheres, more or less firmly, to the content of his conscience, he is obliged to follow its dictates, even if the conscience is false, for not to do what one believes is prescribed is to hold a precept in contempt.[15]

This doctrine as proposed here by Saint Albert the Great differs substantially from what had already been proposed by the Franciscan school, as represented by the *Summa Halesiana*. Albert defines conscience as an act; the Franciscans define it as a habit. Albert teaches that conscience, whether true or erroneous, imposes an obligation as long as one is subjectively convinced his conscience is not in error; the Franciscan doctrine is based rather on the morality of the acts dictated by conscience, so that a conscience dictating an evil act would not place an obligation to be obeyed. However, about thirty years later, in the *Summa Theologica,* at least in the terminology, Albert seems to desert his earlier stand on the nature of conscience, and seems to adopt the Franciscan notions, as we shall now see.

This work, which is referred to by Meersseman as the *Summa Theologica altera,*[16] to distinguish it from the *Summa de Creaturis,* which is sometimes called the *Summa Theologica prior,* was written by Saint Albert between 1270 and 1280. Loss of memory, sickness, and death prevented its completion.[17] It is described by Albert himself as a summary of theological questions written for the brethren who were studying and disputing and who did not always have a copy of the original questions.[18]

In this work, the influence of both Saint Thomas and the Franciscan school is evident, but the greatest influence comes from the *Summa Halesiana.* On this point, Meersseman writes:

> It seems that the influence of the *Summa Theologica* of Saint Thomas is not to be excluded. But undoubtedly greater is the influence of the *Summa Theologica* attributed to Alexander of Hales, but which was in fact composed for the greatest part after

his death from fragments collected from many sources. Nevertheless, the quality of this influence has not yet been sufficiently determined; namely, whether it is material or formal, i.e., whether only words, or also doctrine was borrowed, and whether texts that are similar were taken by Albert from the work of Hales, or whether both took them from a common source.[19]

This influence of the *Summa Halesiana* is especially patent in the treatment of the nature of conscience contained in this work of Saint Albert the Great. To point out the similarity between these works, below are listed in two parallel columns some of the objections concerning the nature of conscience found in both works.

(Conscience is not a potency)

Summa Theologica Alberti

Adhus Damascenus: "Conscientia aliquando recta est, et aliquando erronea; aliquando tranquilla, aliquando perturbata; aliquando munda, aliquando immunda"; quorum nihil convenit potentiae animae; ergo conscientia non est animae potentia.

Summa Halesiana

Quia conscientia dicitur erronea, tranquilla et perturbata; sed ista nulli potentiae conveniunt; ergo conscientia non est potentia.[21]

(Conscience is an acquired habit)

Et videtur quod acquisitus; quia aliquando quis habet conscientia de re quam prius non habuit. Et hujus est exemplum: quia dato mandato a principe vel a Deo, aliquis habet conscientiam de trans-

Item, modo potest quis habere conscientiam alicujus rei quam prius non habuit, sicut patet de Judaeis, qui ante dationem Legis non habebant conscientiam de immundis, sed post dationem gressione m a n d a t i quam prius non habuit; quod non posset si naturaliter esset insita; tunc enim haberet se uno modo.

habuerunt vel habere debuerunt; conscientia ergo incipit esse de aliquibus de quibus ante non fuit; sed habitus naturalis semper est de iis de quibus est; ergo . . . [22]

(Conscience is a natural habit)

Rom., 2:14-15: *Cum enim gentes, q u a e legem non habent, naturaliter q u a e legis sunt faciunt, eiusmodi legem non habentes, ipsi sibi sunt lex, qui ostendunt opus legis, scriptum in cordibus suis,* ibi Glossa Augustini: "Etsi gentiles non habeant legem scriptam, habent tamen legem naturalem qua quisque intelligit et sibi conscius est quid sit bonum et quid sit malum." Hujusmodi lex habitus est naturalis. Ergo et conscientia.

Rom., 2:14: *Cum gentes, quae legem n o n habent, naturaliter quae legis sunt faciunt, eiusmodi legem non habentes, ipsi sibi sunt lex,* Glossa: "Etsi gentiles non habeant legem scriptam qua quisque intelligit et sibi conscius est quid sit bonum et quid sit malum"; sed hujusmodi lex naturalis habitus naturalis; ergo et ipsa conscientia, quia ea conscius est quid sit bonum et quid sit malum.[23]

(Conscience is a cognitive habit)

Conscientia d i c i t scientiam: scientia est habitus cognitivus; ergo et conscientia.

Conscientia ponit scientiam; sed scientia determinat habitum cognitivum; ergo et conscientia.

Adhuc, cum dicitur iste est conscius secretorum illius, sensus est, quod cognitive scit ille; et hoc est secundum habitum cognitivum et non motivum; ergo conscientia dicit habitum cognitivum.

Hoc idem arguitur per simile, quia cum dicitur "iste homo est conscius secretorum hujus hominis," sensus est quod iste novit secreta illius. Unde conscius dicitur propter aliquam notitiam

Adhuc 1*Cor.*,4: 4: *Nihil mihi conscius sum, sed non in hoc justificatus sum.* Hoc dixit Apostolus, quia nescivit se esse in peccato secundum habitum cognitivum. Ergo videtur q u o d conscientia habitus cognitivus est.

1*Cor.*,4: 4: *Nihil mihi conscius sum*: non est sensus: "non moveor ad peccatum," sed potius, "non cognosco me esse in peccato"; unde *Glossa* ibidem, "In nullo me rem o r d e t conscientia mea." Quare conscientia non erit habitus motivus, sed potius cognitivus.

communem, et ita conscius ponit cognitionem; ergo et conscientia; ergo est habitus cognitivus.

Adhuc *Eccles.*,7: 23: *Scit enim conscientia tua quia tu crebro maledixisti aliis.* Glossa, ibidem: "Qua iudice n e m o nocens absolvitur." Scire et judicare fiunt secundum habitum cognitivum. Ergo conscientia est habitus cognitivus.[20]

Eccles.,7: 23 *Scit conscientia tua, quia et tu crebro maledixisti aliis,* et ita conscientiae est scire, et ita ut supra. Hoc idem arguitur ex hoc quod dicitur in Glossa: "Qua iudice nemo nocens absolvitur." Ex quo apparet quod iudicare ad conscientiam pertinet; sed iudicare cognoscentis est, et ita ut prius.[24]

This similarity begins to fade in the body of the article in the work of the Dominican. Both in the *Summa Halesiana* and in Bonaventure's writings, conscience is referred to as a faculty under one aspect, and as a habit in another and more commonly used respect, so that conscience is defined as a habit. In his *Summa Theologica,* Albert also discusses two aspects of conscience, the material and the formal. Whereas the Franciscans concluded conscience is a habit because it includes the notion of knowledge, Saint Albert writes that, in its material aspect, conscience is that which is known or knowable, and thus is neither habit nor faculty, but simply a known (*scitum*). Discussing the formal aspect of conscience, Albert combines the two aspects spoken of by the Franciscans. The Dominican writes that, taken formally, conscience is the knowledge which is referred to that which is known (*scientia quae refertur ad scitum*); thus, he concludes, it is a habit in a faculty, or as he calls it, an habitual faculty of the soul.[25]

According to Albert, then, there are two notions involved in the nature of conscience: a habit, and the object of that habit. He refers to the object of the habit as knowledge referred to something known; he refers to the habit as one which is in a faculty of the soul. This faculty, therefore, must be intellectual. Since knowledge pertains to the intellect, the faculty in question is the intellectual faculty. Conscience is, then, as here described by Albert, the habit of the intellect which refers knowledge to something which is known.

Saint Albert attaches to this habit four qualities. He notes that the habit is natural in so far as the knowledge of first principles is innate in us; and acquired, in that conscience can be considered as knowing this or that thing which one person may know and another not know. Conscience as a habit is both cognitive and motivating: cognitive, since it is the habit of the intellect, a speculation; and motivating since it moves the subject to do or not do an act.[26]

The act of this habit is syllogistic reasoning. The habit of first principles, or synderesis, is the major of the syllogism; the minor is furnished by a principle or truth from reason. The conclusion is the act of conscience. He points this out when he describes the relation of the natural law and conscience:

> It must be said that the natural law and conscience differ essentially, but they agree in relation to the same thing, as a principle and the conclusion drawn

do in a syllogism. For natural law is the principle by which conscience is ruled, the principle under which reason assumes data from this or that; and conscience concludes whether the act is to be done or omitted. An example: the natural law says one must not fornicate, nor steal, nor kill; reason assumes this or that act to be fornication or theft or homicide; conscience concludes the act is not to be done.[27]

In the earlier work, the *Summa de Creaturis,* Saint Albert had stated more explicitly that conscience is an act, the conclusion of the practical reason from two premises, of which the major is synderesis and the minor is supplied by reason.[28] It should be noted that there seems to be a contradiction in Albert's works. In the earlier, he wrote that conscience is an act; in the later *Summa Theologica,* he calls it a habitual faculty. However, there is no real contradiction, but rather an adaptation. Albert changed the terminology in the latter work, using that of the Franciscan school; nevertheless, his concept of conscience is not the same as the Franciscan. He continued to hold his earlier position that conscience is an act. This is shown by the fact that Saint Albert, in the *Summa Theologica,* wrote that the conclusion of a syllogism is the act of the habitual faculty which is conscience; the dictate of conscience is a judgment, which is an act. This judgment is the referral of knowledge to a known, of a particular to a universal. Lottin sums this up when he writes that "in the *Summa Theologica,* written after 1270, Saint Albert recasts his conceptions in the sense of the Franciscan school."[29]

In replying to the objections from the beginning of his treatment on conscience, Albert states that conscience is said to be right or wrong, etc., but this arises from what is the object of conscience, and not from conscience itself.[30] Thus, Albert holds that morality is not ascribed to conscience itself as a characteristic, but the note of morality, or calling conscience right or wrong, true or erroneous, enters in by reason of its object. The object, knowledge, is received by conscience; the conscience modifies the knowledge, since it is the nature of conscience to refer knowledge to a known. Thus, by reason of the referral of the knowledge of a particular to a universal, morality is ascribed to conscience. The act of conscience judges about the particular by referring it to the universal, the particular being a datum from reason, the universal being synderesis. Morality, therefore, belong neither to the knowledge itself, nor to the conscience itself, but to the knowledge as received and modified by the act of conscience.

With this, Saint Albert the Great ends his treatment of conscience. He does not discuss the obligations imposed by conscience in the *Summa Theologica*. It seems then, arguing from silence, that we can say he held to his teaching as he developed it in the earlier *Summa de Creaturis*: as long as one is subjectively convinced his conscience is right, he is obliged to obey its dictates. It makes no difference whether or not the conscience is objectively true; even the dictates of an erroneous conscience must be obeyed if one thinks the knowledge he has, supplied by his reason, is correct. Objectively, one's reason can be erroneous, and thus, one could be acting out of ignorance. Consequently, the doctrine of Saint Albert on ignorance as an excusing cause must be considered. Because of the complexity of the Dominican's treatment of ignorance, it is our intention to present a schema of his teaching before giving an explanation.[31]

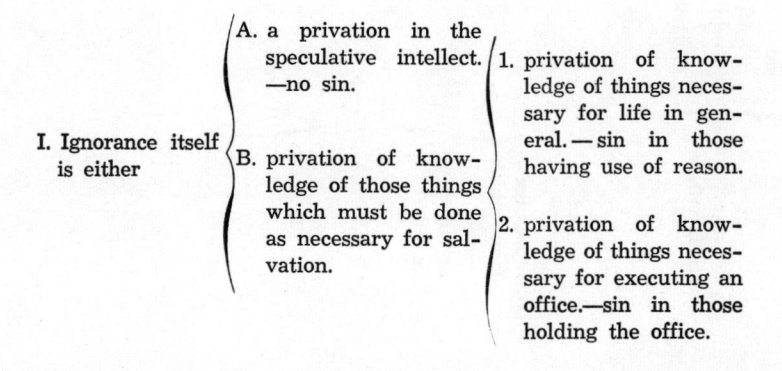

I. Ignorance itself is either
- A. a privation in the speculative intellect. —no sin.
- B. privation of knowledge of those things which must be done as necessary for salvation.
  1. privation of knowledge of things necessary for life in general.—sin in those having use of reason.
  2. privation of knowledge of things necessary for executing an office.—sin in those holding the office.

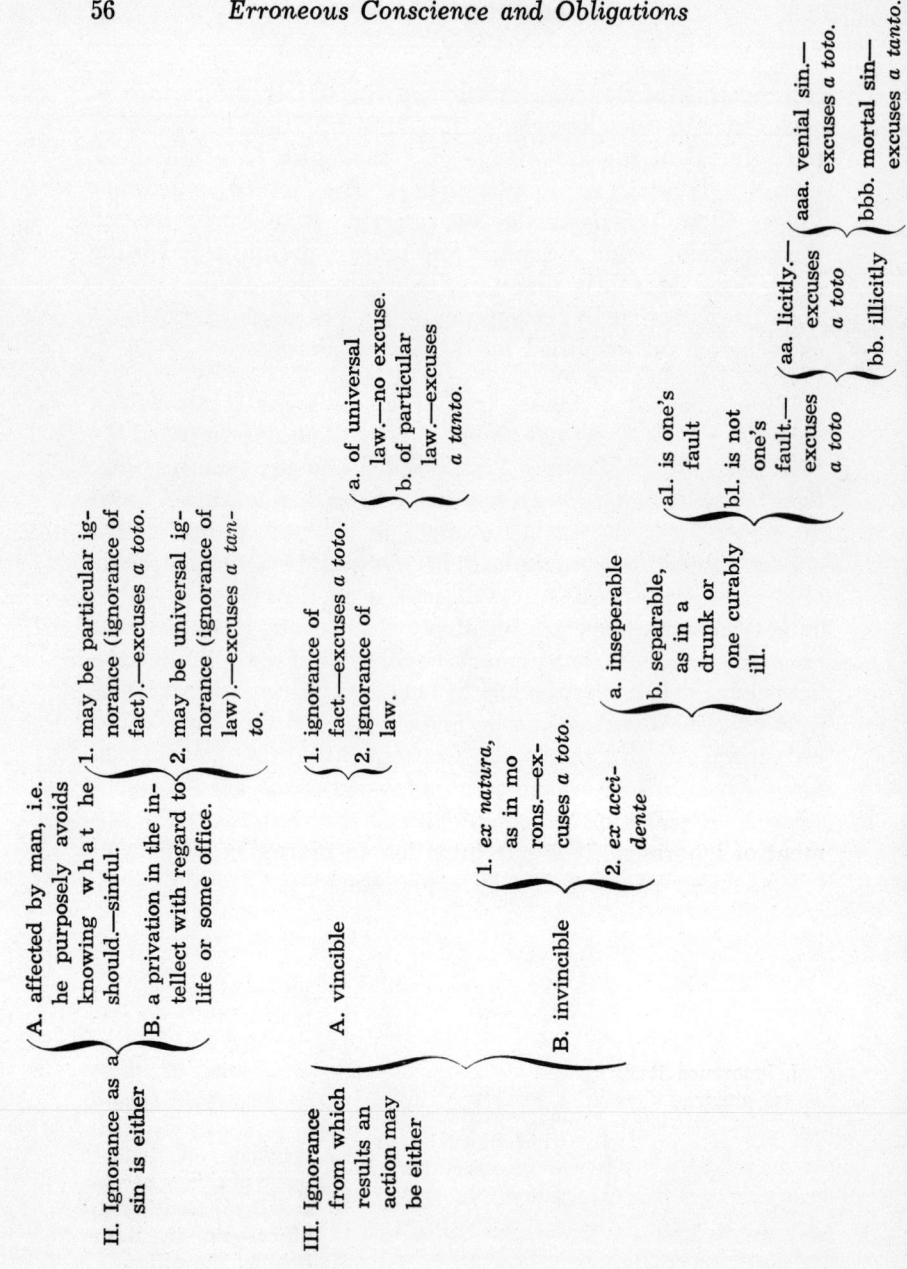

Erroneous Conscience and Obligations

II. Ignorance as a sin is either
- A. affected by man, i.e. he purposely avoids knowing what he should.—sinful.
- B. a privation in the intellect with regard to life or some office.
  - 1. may be particular ignorance (ignorance of fact).—excuses *a toto*.
  - 2. may be universal ignorance (ignorance of law).—excuses *a tanto*.

III. Ignorance from which results an action may be either
- A. vincible
  - 1. ignorance of fact.—excuses *a toto*.
  - 2. ignorance of law.
    - a. of universal law.—no excuse.
    - b. of particular law.—excuses *a tanto*.
- B. invincible
  - 1. *ex natura*, as in morons.—excuses *a toto*.
  - 2. *ex accidente*
    - a. inseperable
    - b. separable, as in a drunk or one curably ill.
      - a1. is one's fault
      - b1. is not one's fault.—excuses *a toto*
        - aa. licitly.—excuses *a toto*
        - bb. illicitly
          - aaa. venial sin.—excuses *a toto*.
          - bbb. mortal sin—excuses *a tanto*.

This summary may seem a little labored and confusing to modern theological minds, but this is inevitable because of the treatment of ignorance by Saint Albert the Great. His divisions and distinctions are not completely disjunctive, and this may be the cause of some of the difficulty. It should be remembered also, that in the thirteenth century, theological thought was in the process of development; theological syntheses were being formulated. Scholastic doctrine on ignorance was in the formative stage; it was not yet fully developed and solidified.

As for the first part of Albert's doctrine, it deals with ignorance itself, objectively. He defines ignorance as a privation of knowledge. This privation is sinful if one should have the knowledge; therefore, the ignorance of the moral truths necessary for salvation, (e.g., that fornication is a mortal sin,) is sinful in all those who have the use of reason. Ignorance of those things necessary for some office, e.g., ignorance of those things without which the sacerdotal office cannot be fulfilled, is sinful for those who hold the office. If, however, the privation is only in the speculative intellect, there is no sin.[32]

In the second part of the schema, the mode in which ignorance is sinful is discussed. From the conclusions drawn and the language used, it seems that Saint Albert is speaking here of ignorance in the subjective order. Whereas before, he wrote that ignorance of law is sinful, in this section, he says that such ignorance excuses. He writes that ignorance which is only affected, i.e., man purposely avoids knowing what he should know, is sinful, and consequently, any act done as a result of this type of ignorance is imputed to the agent. Ignorance in the practical intellect may be either particular ignorance, ignorance of fact, which provides a total excuse for an act resulting from it, or it may be universal ignorance, ignorance of law, which provides a partial excuse. Albert gives as a reason for this that such ignorance is the cause of involuntariness, which merits some pardon and mercy.[33]

The third division of the schema deals with ignorance as an excuse for a resulting action's not being imputed to the agent. Saint Albert divides ignorance, in this regard, into two main categories, vincible and invincible. Vincible ignorance, he writes, may be either ignorance of fact, which is a total excuse, or ignorance of law. According to whether the law is universal or particular, ignorance is or is not an excusing cause. If one is ignorant of a universal law, the knowledge of which is imposed on all, this offers no excuse. Since everyone is held to know this law, ignorance of it is a sin of omission, and excuses no one. However, if the ignorance is of some particular law, which is known only through study, then such ignorance excuses according to the degree of difficulty involved in the study.[34]

Invincible ignorance,[35] in the structure of Albert's teaching, is either natural, as for example, in morons or in those naturally stupid, and this is a total excuse, or the ignorance is accidental. This accidental invincible ignorance is divided and subdivided by Saint Albert without much explanation. Such ignorance, writes the Doctor, is either separable or inseparable. Because he describes separable ignorance as that which is present in one who is drunk or curably ill, it seems logical to conclude that by inseparable and separable ignorance, Saint Albert means this type of ignorance arises from some "accident," as distinguished from "natural" ignorance, and the effects of the accident can be either permanent (inseparable) or transient (separable). Thus, it seems that inseparable accidental ignorance would be that which is present in one who loses the use of his reason because of some other cause than a natural one, which cause has permanent damaging effects, such as an incurable and painful disease.

Separable ignorance, or that present in one who is drunk or curably ill, is subdivided according to whether the cause was the fault of the agent or not. If it were not imputable to the agent, as when one did not know the strength of the wine he was drinking, the ignorance would be a total excuse for a subsequent action. On the other hand, if the cause were the fault of the agent, then there must be a further subdivision. Either he acted lawfully or unlawfully. In the event that his action was lawful, the resulting ignorance is a total excuse for a subsequent action, because the action is simply involuntary. Though Albert gives no example of this, it seems we can visualize a case where one could lawfully bring about the state described by the Saint: a man about to undergo surgery can take a strong stimulating drink to deaden the pain in the absence of anaesthesia. He would then be drunk through his own fault, and lawfully so. If, on the other hand, the action of the agent was unlawful, then there is a final subdivision into whether the action was a venial or a mortal sin. Were it a venial sin, a subsequent action resulting from the ignorance would not be imputed; the ignorance offers a total excuse; but if the action were a mortal sin, the ignorance offers a partial excuse, though both the ignorance and the subsequent action are imputed to the agent.[36]

In capsule form, it can be said that Saint Albert the Great teaches that ignorance which is voluntary is no excuse for a subsequent action, and involuntary ignorance is an excuse, either totally or partially, according to the degree of involuntariness involved. This is borne out by his replies to objecions raised by him in the acticles cited, in which he gives his answer that if ignorance is voluntary, it is sinful, as well as by the fact that in his exposition of ignorance cited above, each time he gives a reason for saying that ignorance excuses, the reason is because the ignorance is a cause of involuntariness.

Thus, the teaching of Saint Albert the Great on conscience and its obligations can be better understood when it is considered in the light of his teaching on ignorance. As was stated previously, Saint Albert teaches that one must follow the dictates of his conscience as long as he is subjectively convinced his conscience is a true one. This subjective state is verified when the agent has opinion, faith, or knowledge. If these are objectively true, his conscience is a true conscience; if they are objectively false, however, his conscience is erroneous. In this latter case, he must obey his conscience if the ignorance resulting in the error is involuntary; and thus, an evil act, performed or a good act omitted in accordance with such a conscience is not imputed to the agent.[37] If the ignorance is voluntary, then the action or omission dictated by conscience is imputed, or excused only to a degree, on the basis of the teaching of Saint Albert the Great on ignorance.[38]

FOOTNOTES

1. Lottin dates this work around 1240-41. See Lottin, O, O. S. B., "La nature de la conscience morale," *ETL* 9 (1932) 265. Meersseman also places the *Summa de Creaturis* prior to the *Summa Theologica*. See Meersseman, P. G., O. P., *Introductio in Opera Omnia B. Alberti Magni* (Baeyart, Belgium, 1931) 107.

2. Lottin, *art. cit.*, 266, notes that this *Summa* was written after 1270.

3. Gilson, E., *History of Christian Philosophy in the Middle Ages* (Random House, New York, 1955) 278.

4. See Meersseman, *op. cit.*, 107.

5. Lottin describes the definition of synderesis according to Saint Albert as a faculty or power coupled with a habit, which furnishes man with the principles of the natural law: *synderesis est vis cum habitu principiorum iuris naturalis*. Synderesis confines itself to the abstract, to generalities; it is not a motion from the will, but a directive emanating from the reason. Thus, synderesis does not act in the order of efficient causality, but in that of the formal cause, dictating to conscience the fundamental norms of moral conduct. Its functions are to judge good and evil in general, incline to the good, and repudiate the evil.—See Lottin, *Psychologie et morale* 2.1, 212-14.

6. *Summa de Creaturis*, II, q. 72, a.1, sol. (ed. Borget, *Opera Omnia*, 35, 1896) 599.

7. *Loc. cit.*

8. See Lottin, *Psychologie et morale*, 217.

9. Qui facit contra conscientiam aedificat ad gehennam.—*Summa de Creaturis, ibid.*, a.2, ob.1, 600. This is a statement from Innocent III. See Prümmer, D., O. P., *Manuale Theologiae Moralis* 1 (ed. 13, Herder, Rome, 1958) 199, footnote 19. The statement is found in the Decretals of Gregory, c. 13, X 2, 13.

10. Si conscientia dictet aliquid esse faciendum per modum precepti, quod tamen non sit praeceptum, si non facit, contemnit quantum in se est praecipientem et praeceptum. Omne autem contemnens praeceptum peccat mortaliter. Ergo iste peccat mortaliter; ergo obligatur ad faciendum; et noniisi ex conscientia; ergo conscientia obligat ad faciendum.—*Summa de Creaturis, loc. cit.*, a.2, 2.

11. *Ibid.*, ad 1, 601.

12. *Ibid.*, ad 2.

13. Est dubitatio indeterminatus motus rationis super utramque partem contradictionis. Ambiguitas autem est motus rationis ambiens utramque partem contradictionis per aequalia media. Opinio vero est acceptio unius partis cum formidine alterius . . . ; scientia est eorum quae cognoscuntur per causam et quoniam impossibile est aliter se habere.—*ibid.*, q. 53, a.1, 447.

14. Ad id quod ulterius quaeritur solvendum, recolendum est distinctio quam supra posuimus: scilicet quod aliud est dubium, et aliud est ambiguum, et aliud persuasum vel creditum, et aliud scitum . . . . Unde quod est in conscientia habet se per aliquem istorum modorum, et secundum hoc magis et minus obligat: sed sine praeiudicio loquendo dicimus, quod non obligat ad faciendum, nisi sit ut opinatum, vel creditum, vel scitum id quod est in conscientia, et tunc obligat, sive conscientia sit erronea, sive ratio erronea: et hoc propter contemptum, sicut probat objectio.—*ibid.*, q. 72, a. 2, 601.

15. See Lottin, *Psychologie et morale*, 387.

16. See Meersseman, *op. cit.*, 111.

17. *Ibid.*, 112.

18. *Opera Omnia Alberti Magni* 33 (ed. Bornget, 1895) 402.

19. Influxus *Summae Theologicae S. Thomae* non omnino excludendus videtur. Major tamen et indubitabilis videtur influxus *Summae Theologicae quae Alexandri Halensis dicitur,* sed de facto maxima pro parte eo mortuo conflata fuit ex fragmentis undique collectis. Attamen, non iam satis determinata est qualitas, ut dicam, hujus influxus; utrum nempe sit materialis vel formalis, i.e., utrum verba tantum, an etiam doctrina mutuata fuit ex ea; et utrum textus similes ab Alberto transsumpti sunt ex Halensi, vel ab utroque e communi fonte.—Meersseman, *op. cit.*, 112-3. See also Gorce, M., O. P., "Le probleme des trois sommes," *RT* 36 (1931) 293-7.

20. *Summa Theologica B. Alberti*, II, tr. 14, q. 99, mem.3, a.1 (ed. Bornget, *Opera Omnia*, 33, 1895) 240-41.

21. *Summa Halesiana*, 2, n. 421, p. 496.

22. *Ibid.*, n. 422, p. 497.

23. *Loc. cit.*

24. *Ibid.*, n. 423, pp. 497-8.

25. *Summa Theologica Alberti*, loc. cit., 241.

26. *Ibid.*, 241-2.

27. Dicendum quod lex naturalis et conscientia differunt per essentiam, sed conveniunt in ordine ad idem, sicut in syllogismis principium et illata conclusio. Lex enim naturalis principium est quo regitur conscientia, sub quo principio ratio assumit de hoc et de illo; et conscientia concludit de faciendo vel non faciendo. Ut sic verbi gratia, lex naturalis dicit esse non fornicandum, nec furandum, nec occidendum, ratio assumit hoc vel illud esse fornicationem vel furtum vel homicidium, conscientia concludit non esse faciendum.— *ibid.*, a.2, 244.

28. See above, pp. 45-6.

29. Lottin, "La nature de la conscience morale," 266.

30. *Summa Theologica Alberti*, loc. cit., 241.

31. The sources for this schema will be indicated along with the explanation of the schema in the following pages.

32. See *In II Sent.*, d. 22, a. 7, sol. (ed. Borgnet, *Opera Omnia*, 27, 18) 382-3; *Summa Theologica*, II, tr. 14, q. 88, sol. 160.61; Bertke, *The Possibility of Ignorance*, 54-5.

33. The teaching of Saint Albert on ignorance is rather confusing to a modern mind; therefore, here is given the full text from which the second part of the schema is taken.

Ignorantia secundum quod est peccatum, sive de se sive de annexo, aliquid habet in affectu, secundum quod affectata dicitur; et habet aliquid in intellectu, scilicet privationem habitus regentis in operabilibus pertinentibus ad vitam vel officium. Dicendum igitur quod quantum ad primum peccatum est. Quantum autem ad secundum non est peccatum et excusat vel a toto si est particularis et facti; vel a tanto, si est iuris vel universalis, quod idem est; quia ex illa parte facit ignorare circumstantias in quibus est actus, et ita est causa involuntarii quod meretur ignoscentiam et misericordiam aliquam. *In II Sent.*, d. 22, a. 9, sol., 385; see also *Summa Theologica*, loc. cit.* Saint Albert, in accord with other theologians, calls ignorance of fact particular ignorance because it is ignorance of a particular fact which even a learned person could possibly not know; he uses the example of Jacob's not knowing he received Lia in place of Rachel. Ignorance of law is called universal ignorance, because law is considered as the universal norms which

rule life or the conducting of an office.—*Ignorantia iuris et facti
. . . est idem quod Theologi vocant universalem et particularem:
quia ius vocatur hic regulae universales et regentes vitam vel
officium. Factum autem, hoc particulare vel illud, quod contingit
etiam sapientem ignorare; sicut Jacob ignoravit sibi suppositam
Liam pro Rachele (Gen. 29:16).—In II Sent.*, d. 22, a. 10, sol., 387.

34. It seems that in today's theological concepts, this universal or particular law referred to by Albert are the primary or secondary precepts of the natural law.

35. The terms vincible and invincible in Albert's writing do not coincide with the meanings attributed to them in theological works today. Invincible ignorance is described by Prümmer as that which cannot be overcome even with the use of moral diligence; vincible is that which can be so overcome, but is not, either because of negligence or ill will. See Prümmer, *Manuale*, 34; Regatillo, E. F. and Zalba, M., S. J., *Theologiae Moralis Summa* 1 (B. A. C., Matriti, 1952) 105.

36. See *In II Sent.*, d. 22, a. 10, sol., 387; *Summa Theologica*, II, tr. 14, q. 88, sol., 160-61. For the sake of clarity, and to indicate the difficulties involved in this treatment of ignorance by Albert, the complete text from the *Commentary on the Sentences* referred to above is given here.

Ignorantia quandoque dividitur secundum causam efficientem . . . in vincibilem et invicibilem et haec divisio est multiplex. Est enim invincibilis ex natura, et haec in toto excusat, qualis est in naturaliter stultis, morionibus, et melancholicis. Et est invincibilis ex accidente: quae duplex est quoniam illud accidens aut separabile aut inseparabile. Si separabile: aut est ex oppilante aliquo vias spiritus animalis in cerebro et turbante organum a quo species accipit ratio; vel ab accidente infirmitatis inseparabilis et insanabilis. Et primo modo est modo est in ebrio vel eo qui jusquiamum, vel opium, vel aliquid aliud bibit. Secundo modo est in infirmo; et sic distinguitur in causa: quia aut ipse dedit operam, aut non. Si non, ut si fuit ignarus qualitatis vini, vel ejus quod sumpsit, tunc in toto excusat eum. Si autem ipse dedit operam, aut per rem licitam aut illicitam. Si primo modo, iterum in toto excusatur etiamsi aliquid postea male agit. Si autem per rem illicitam: aut illa fuit veniale peccatum aut mortale. Si primo modo adhuc excusat in toto. Si secundo modo, non in toto, meo iudicio, excusat, sed in parte. . . . Si autem est vincibilis: tunc dividitur ulterius penes materiam in ignorantiam iuris et facti, et hoc est idem quod theologi vocant universalem et particularem, quia jus vocatur hic regulae universales et regentes vitam vel officium; factum autem, hoc particulare vel illud, quod contingit etiam sapientem ignorare, . . . et ideo (ignorantia facti) in toto excusat. Juris autem est duplex: quia quoddam est jus universale, quod omnibus imponitur ad sciendum; et quoddam est particulare, quod non scitur nisi per studium: et puto, quod prima est crassa et supina, non excusans. Secundo autem excusat a tanto.

By comparing this text with that quoted in footnote 33 the difficulties involved in interpreting Albert will be made clear to the reader.

37. This doctrine is somewhat parallel to the modern teaching on invincibly erroneous conscience. Saint Albert's teaching on voluntary ignorance closely parallels today's teaching on a vincibly erroneous conscience.

38. Saint Albert does not discuss the question of the possibility of gaining merit by following an erroneous conscience. This problem, discussed by the Franciscans, is taken up again by Saint Albert's pupil, Saint Thomas Aquinas, and will be discussed at some length in the next chapter.

CHAPTER 4

SAINT THOMAS AQUINAS

§1 INTRODUCTION

With the appearance of his Commentary on the Sentences around 1254,[1] Saint Thomas Aquinas entered the scene in which the question of conscience was being discussed. Thomas took up and developed the thoughts of his teacher, Saint Albert the Great. The thoughts expressed by Aquinas in this work signalled a divergence which would reach its maturity when his doctrine was fully developed twenty years later at his death. Saint Bonaventure, who died in the same year as Thomas,[2] developed the thought of the Franciscan School, and it can be said that in 1274, the teaching on conscience and its obligations as taught by the Franciscans was differed substantially from the Dominican doctrine. Just as the Seraphic Doctor developed the teaching of the *Summa Halesiana*, so did the Angelic Doctor develop the teaching of Saint Albert, clarifying it, explaining it, and, even in some instances, correcting it.

§2 THE NATURE OF CONSCIENCE

Saint Thomas was aware of the doctrine proposed by the Franciscans, as he showed when he wrote that conscience is generally understood in various ways. It may be that of which one is conscious, the habit by which one is conscious, or the faculty which has this consciousness.[3] This is evidently a reference to the teaching of the *Summa Halesiana*.[4] Aquinas immediately rejects these proposals, claiming they are improperly applied to conscience. He writes that conscience is that which binds or burdens one, and since no one is bound to do anything unless he considers the obligation first, there must be some actual consideration of reason through conscience.[5] He then discusses in what this consideration of reason consists, and here the influence of his teacher is apparent.

Thomas accepts Albert's interpretation of Aristotle that reason uses syllogisms when it makes a choice, and also his application of this to conscience.[6] Aquinas writes:

> Reason, when choosing or rejecting, uses syllogisms. In syllogisms, there is a threefold consideration, according to the three premises, of which the third is concluded from the other two. Thus it also happens in the proposed situation (i.e. conscience), since reason, in working from universal principles, makes a judgment about particulars. Since universal principles of law pertain to synderesis, and since more appropriate reasons for a work pertain to habits by which superior and inferior reason are distinguished, synderesis in this syllogism is that which proposes the major premise (the consideration of which is the act of synderesis), and the minor is proposed by the superior or inferior reason (and its consideration is the act of reason). The consideration of the conclusion drawn is the consideration of conscience.[7]

The conclusion of a syllogism, then, is the act of conscience. Thomas adds a note not found in Saint Albert, that it is the duty of conscience both to upbraid one for something already done and speak out against an act about to be done.[8] Conscience applies universal knowledge to some particular act, and thus conscience is said to be *quasi cum alio scientia*. It is easily seen then that conscience is a dictate of reason, an act. Saint Thomas takes this occasion to point out also that conscience can err because reason can err, and reason plays a major role in conscience.[9] He also indicates that conscience differs from the natural law and from synderesis.

> Natural law designates those universal principles of law; synderesis designates their habit, or their habitual faculty; conscience designates a certain application of the natural law to an act to be done, by way of a conclusion (of a syllogism).[10]

Having described conscience as a judgment resulting from a syllogism, the Angelic Doctor then describes the nature of this judgment as cognitive. The judgment which is conscience is a particular judgment, which is limited by knowledge, and thus conscience is a cognitive conclusion of a particular thing to be done.[11] Thus, conscience is the application of the first law, that good is to be done and evil avoided, to particular acts about to be performed.[12]

In his later works, the Angelic Doctor again discusses the nature of conscience, but he never deviates from this position as stated in his Commentary on the Sentences. He amplifies and solidifies his position by adding considerations and answering objections, all aimed at demonstrating that conscience is an act of syllogistic reasoning which tells one the morality of an act already placed or about to be placed.

The next work in which Saint Thomas speaks of the nature of conscience is the *De Veritate,* written between 1256 and 1259.[13] Before studying what the Doctor wrote in this work, it would be well to point out the following observation made by Dom Lottin:

> The *De Veritate* brings a few developments. The current language, the norm of precision in matter of terminology, will serve as a point of departure. Ordinary language uses indifferently certain words, such as "intellect" to designate at the same time the act, the faculty from which the act emanates, and the habitual disposition which inclines towards that act . . . . On the contrary, the word "conscience" is not used except to signify the act of conscience. Why this difference? The same word is applied to the act and to the faculty from which it emanates when the act is proper to that faculty, and so it is with the words "intellect, sight." But it also happens that an act belongs indifferently to several faculties; such as the act by which the faculty is applied to an action, e.g.,

"usus." . . . The same is applied to the word "conscience." For the word "conscience" . . . does not imply any faculty, nor any special habit of knowledge of which conscience would be the proper act. The "knowledge" is, in effect, . . . *any* knowledge (*quaecumque notitia*).[14]

Thus, conscience is used by Saint Thomas to indicate only the act of the practical reason, the application of knowledge to a particular act. In this work, he amplifies this point of his doctrine. This application of knowledge to a particular act can be done in two ways: one can consider whether or not an act was done, or whether an act is right or wrong. According to the first way, one is said to be conscious of an act, in as much as he knows it has or has not been performed. This conscience is said to testify, and it is not the moral conscience, but is is called the psychological conscience.[15]

According to the second manner of application, i.e., considering whether an act is right or wrong, there are two possibilities. Through the habit of knowledge and its applications, we can be directed to do or not do something, and this practical judgment is similar to discovery, i.e., to speculative knowledge by which we proceed from principles to conclusions. The other possibility is to examine an act already done, to judge whether an act was right or wrong, and this is similar to speculative judgment through which we reduce conclusions to principles.

Thomas notes that conscience is used in both these meanings. When knowledge is applied to an act, directing the act to be done or omitted, conscience is said to prod or bind us. When knowledge is applied to an act by way of examination of its morality, then conscience accuses or causes remorse or approves.[16]

Aquinas raises an objection against his contention that conscience is an act: conscience does not always exist, e.g., in one who is asleep, and therefore, it cannot be an act. He replies that the act, though not always existing, nevertheless remains in its principle, i.e., it remains radically in habits which are applicable to act.[17] By these habits applicable to act, the Angelic Doctor is referring to the habits of synderesis, wisdom, and knowledge:

... by the application (of knowledge to an act), by which we take counsel about that which should be done, or examine what has already been done, the operative habits of reason are applied to an act. These are the habit of synderesis and the habit of wisdom, by which the higher reason is perfected, and the habit of scientific knowledge, which perfects lower reason. Of these, either all are applied at the same time, or only one of them is applied. With these habits we examine what we have done and, according to these habits, we take counsel about what should be done.[18]

These habits are always present in man, and, radically present in these habits as operative, is the act which is produced when some knowledge is referred to the universal in regard to a particular act.

The *Summa Theologica* of Saint Thomas also gives us material from which we can gather his doctrine on the nature of conscience. In the first part, written sometime after 1265,[19] Aquinas gives two demonstrations which show that conscience is an act. The first demonstration is developed from the very term. Conscience (*cum scientia*) imports the order of knowledge to something else, for it is knowledge with another.[20] It is only by some act that knowledge can be applied to something, and therefore, conscience, which does this applying, must be an act.

From those things which are attributed to conscience according to the ordinary manner of speaking, Thomas gives a second demonstration that conscience is an act. Conscience is said to testify, bind, instigate, excuse, accuse, or cause remorse. These only follow from the application of some knowledge to that which one does, and this application can be done in any of three ways. One can recognize what has been done or not done, and this is to testify. One can judge whether some act is to be done or not, and this is to instigate or bind. And lastly, an act already performed can be judged as right or wrong, and this is to excuse, accuse, or cause remorse. All these follow the actual application of knowledge to that which is done, and consequently, conscience, which applies this knowledge, is an act.[21]

Summing up what Saint Thomas teaches about the nature of conscience, we can see that he consistently taught it was an act of the practical intellect, the conclusion of a syllogism, the major of which is from synderesis, and the minor from reason. This act is a judgment about some action already performed or about an action about to be performed. In this dissertation, we are concerned only about conscience as a judgment concerning an action about to be performed, since only this is a norm of morality. It can also be noted that Saint Thomas and Saint Bonaventure both refer to conscience as a judgment of the practical reason. Bonaventure dissents from Aquinas in what L. Rodrigo calls a secondary matter, namely, whether conscience is principally a habit, as claimed by the Franciscan, or rather an act, as the Dominican taught.[22] This judgment, which is conscience, concerns the morality of the act about to be performed, for, as Thomas indicates, the moral conscience can consider whether an act is right or wrong, whether it should be performed or omitted.[23] Thus, conscience is a norm of morality; it judges the morality of some particular action.

§3 THE OBLIGATION IMPOSED BY CONSCIENCE

This judgement is, however, a fallible one, i.e., conscience can make mistaken judgments. Aquinas once again follows the path indicated by his teacher when he writes that principles supplied by reason can be the cause of error in the syllogism which results in the act of conscience. Since the truth of the conclusion depends both upon the major and the minor of the syllogism, it follows that if there is error, it is in one of these premises, or it results from a false syllogism.[24] Now, the major is supplied by synderesis, but these principles are known naturally and *per se* and no error is possible in these. The minor is supplied by reason; these determined principles are not known *per se,* but rather through the searchings of reason, which is sometimes deceived; therefore, error enters into conscience through these principles supplied by reason or through a neglect of the proper forms of syllogization.[25]

Thomas also distinguishes error which is proper to conscience and error which results from some choice:

> In a conclusion of a particular thing to be done, there are two ways in which there can be a defect. One way is from the falsity of the principles from which the syllogism is built, and in this way, what is contrary to truth is found in the conclusion; this is an error of conscience. The other way arises from the impetus of the passions which absorb and, in a sense, bind the judgment of reason in some particular act, so that it considers neither the act nor its opposite, but the will seeks the delight proposed by the senses; this is an error of choice, not of conscience.[26]

Thus, conscience is a judgment which can err about the morality of an act about to be performed. The next question which logically follows concerns the obligation imposed on the agent by this judgment. Must he follow this judgment; if so, is the obligation absolute, since the judgment can be wrong? The Angelic Doctor replies to these questions in various works, and by studying his answers, chronologically, there can be seen a process of clarification and solidification of his thought. His principal argument is found in its essentials in the first of his writings dealing with this question, the Commentary on the Sentences, and Thomas uses the same argument in his later works, refining and strengthening it. It is our intention to develop his argument as he himself did, following the chronological order of his works, developing simultaneously the replies to these questions: does conscience oblige; how; what of erroneous conscience? After the exposition of the development of the teachings of Saint Thomas, a summary of his doctrine will be given.

In the Commentary on the Sentences, Aquinas notes that there are two opinions on the obligations of conscience. The first is that which claims there is an obligation imposed according to the intrinsic morality of the act dictated by conscience, an obvious reference to the teaching of the Franciscans. Thomas rejects this opinion, embracing rather the other.

He writes:

> If one diligently investigates how conscience binds, it will be found to oblige in all things, as another opinion claims. For conscience is a certain dictate of reason. Now the will is not moved to seek anything, unless some apprehension of that thing is presupposed, for the object of the will is good or evil according as it is imagined or understood . . . . Since the act of the will is specified by its object, it is necessary that the act of the will be according to the judgment of reason and conscience, and in this way, conscience is said to oblige: for if anyone, through his will, should flee from what the reason dictates as good, this is a flight from good, which flight is evil, because the will flees it as if it were good according to the reason . . . ; likewise, if the reason dictates some good as evil, the will cannot tend to it without being evil, for it tends to it as it is presented by the reason . . . . Therefore, whether reason or conscience judges right-

ly or not, the will is obliged in this way, that if the act of the will does not follow the judgment or dictate of reason, which is conscience, it is inordinate; and this is to oblige, namely, to bind the will, so that it cannot tend to something else without harm of deformity.[27]

Thus, Thomas follows in the footsteps of his master, Saint Albert. Whereas the master spoke of obligation as long as one was subjectively convinced that his conscience was right, the pupil reaches the same conclusion by speaking of the will's being moved by good, not objective good, but good as presented by the reason. When the reason apprehends something as good, and issues a dictate to the will, the will is obliged to follow this dictate; otherwise the will is inordinate. Therefore, conscience, whether true or erroneous, binds.[28] However, Saint Thomas adds immediately that there is a difference in the obligation imposed by a true conscience and an erroneous one. A true conscience obliges *per se* and *simpliciter,* for that which is dictated is good in itself and it appears good. An erroneous conscience, on the other hand, only obliges *per accidens* and *secundum quid;* its dictate is only an apprehended good, and therefore this good only obliges as apprehended.[29]

Saint Thomas then makes a statement which seems to put him on the side of the Franciscans. He writes:

> If one should do an act which is in itself evil, but which erroneous reason judges to be good, sin is not avoided; but if one does not do the act, sin is incurred, since a single defect of goodness is sufficient for an act to be evil, whether the goodness which is lacking is accidental, in as much as the act is apprehended under the aspect of goodness, or whether the goodness (lacking) is essential to the act. However, if (the defect) be of the former only, i.e., only accidental, the act will not be good on this account.[30]

It would seem from this text that Saint Thomas agrees with the Franciscan position that one is in a quandary when his erroneous conscience dictates an act. Even his reply to the objection that one would be in a quandary reflects the Franciscan position, for Thomas says that one is really not in a quandary in this case, for he can set aside such a conscience, since it is erroneous.[31] Thus, Thomas says on the one hand, that one must follow his erroneous conscience since it commands an apparent good, and on the other hand, man sins by following the dictates of an erroneous conscience. Basing ourselves on the axiom that Saint Thomas is his own best interpreter, we will postpone comment on this seeming paradox until the reasoning process of Aquinas is further developed.

An answer to another objection will throw further light on the ideas of Saint Thomas on the obligatory force of conscience. He writes that conscience does not oblige by its own power (*virtus*), but rather in virtue of a divine precept. Conscience does not command something because it seems it should be done, but because it is prescribed by God, i.e., in as much as conscience says this thing is commanded by God, it must be done.[32]

In the *De Veritate,* Aquinas again discusses the question of the obligation imposed by conscience. To clarify his explanation, he points out that the term "binding" as far as spiritual entities are concerned is used metaphorically. In the physical order, binding means the imposition of necessity, e.g., one who is bound necessarily stays in the place where he is bound. This necessity is imposed from without. Now such necessity can be imposed in either of two ways: either by force, or by a conditional necessity, e.g., if one does not do such a thing, he will not receive a reward. Necessity by force cannot affect the will, since the will is naturally free from force; the other, however, can be imposed on the will. This necessity is only imposed on the will by some action, and this action is the command of a superior. The command itself cannot induce the will to act unless the command reaches the one to be commanded, and this is done through knowledge. Therefore, no one is bound by any precept unless he has, or should have, knowledge of that precept. By the same power (*virtus*) that a precept binds, conscience also binds, since a precept does not bind except in virtue of the knowledge, and knowledge does not bind except in virtue of the precept. Thus, since conscience is the application of knowledge to an act, conscience binds in virtue of a divine precept.[33]

Consequently, it is easily seen that Saint Thomas is clarifying his earlier teaching that the obligation of conscience depends on the good as apprehended by the reason. What is apprehended as good by the reason and presented to the will moves the will to act. This apprehension of good is knowledge.

The conditional obligation imposed by conscience, according to Aquinas, is that unless the conscience is obeyed, one sins.[34] By way of refutation of the Franciscan doctrine, he notes that conscience is not said to oblige simply because one does right in following it; otherwise a counsel would be said to be obligatory.[35]. Again attacking the position of the Franciscans, Saint Thomas writes:

> It does not seem possible for a man to avoid sin if his conscience, no matter how mistaken, declares that something which is indifferent or intrinsically evil is a command of God, and with such a conscience, he decides to do the opposite. For, as far as he can, he has by this very fact, decided not to observe the law of God. Consequently, he sins mortally. Accordingly, although such a false conscience can be changed, nevertheless, as long as it remains, it is binding, since one who acts against it necessarily commits a sin.[36]

Thus, conscience obliges because it is a judgment of the practical reason which tells one that an action is in accordance with or is contrary to the law of God. If man does not heed his conscience, he willingly acts contrary to what he believes is the divine law, and consequently, sins. However, as he did before, Aquinas immediately draws a distinction between the mode of obligation imposed by a true and an erroneous conscience. Formerly, he had written that a true conscience obliges *per se* and *simpliciter* because what it dictated appeared good and was objectively good.[37] In this work, the Angelic Doctor adds to this explanation, that a true conscience binds *simpliciter* because the obligation is absolute and present in every event. One cannot set aside such a conscience without sin and one cannot disobey its dictates without sin; therefore, it obliges *per se* and *simpliciter*.[38]

In a similar vein, he further explains the obligation of the erroneous conscience: it obliges only *secundum quid* and conditionally, i.e., as long as the conscience remains. One can set aside its dictates without sin, and therefore, an erroneous conscience does not oblige in every event. One who adheres to his false conscience, believing it to be a true one clings to it because of the correctness he believes is there, and strictly speaking, he adheres to a true conscience which is false *quasi per accidens*, i.e., in so far as this conscience which he believes to be true happens to be false.[39]

Soon after the writing of the *De Veritate*, Saint Thomas finished other works in which he again discusses the obligation of conscience. The later works make his doctrine more precise, and, as it were, put the final touches on his reasoning. These works include *Quodlibetales* 8 and 3, the *Prima-Secundae* of the *Summa Theologica*, and his *Commentary on Saint Paul's Epistle to the Romans*. The *Commentary on the Epistle* seems to be the last of these works. Walz, basing himself on Mandonnet and Grabmann, dates this work in 1272-2.[40] The same authority dates the *Prima Secundae* at 1269-70; Eschmann also gives this date.[41] However, there does not seem to be agreement as to a date for the writing of the *Quodlibetalis* 8. Though both Eschmann and Walz give 1269-72 for *Quodlibetales* 1 to 6,[42] they disagree as to the others. Eschmann dates them between 1256 and 1259.[43] Walz, however, places them later, between 1265 and 1267.[44] This problem of chronolgy would not affect our treatment of the question of conscience, since, at any rate, *Quodlibetalis* 8 would be the first of these works which are still to be treated.

Quodlibetalis 8 presents a special difficulty to our problem. We have seen thus far that Saint Thomas taught that erroneous conscience obliges. In the *Commentary on the Sentences,* he wrote that it is a sin to follow and a sin not to follow an erroneous conscience.[45] In the *De Veritate,* he wrote that conscience is said to oblige because one sins by disobeying its commands, and that an erroneous conscience obliges as long as it is not set aside. In this work, Thomas writes "that which is done contrary to the law is always evil, nor is it excused by the fact that it is according to conscience. Likewise, what is contrary to conscience is evil, even though it is not contrary to the law."[46]

This statement deepens the problem surrounding the doctrine of Saint Thomas on the obligations of an erroneous conscience. It appears he is teaching that one is obliged to sin. At this point in our exposition of the teaching of the Angelic Doctor, we are not prepared to attempt a solution to this paradox. It is our intention to complete first the statement of the teaching of Aquinas in order that a more complete picture may be had, into which can be fitted the various aspects. This problem cannot be adequately solved without a full presentation of the doctrine of Thomas on the obligations of conscience and the effect of ignorance on those obligations. Therefore, the discussion of this problem will be left until a later portion of this chapter.

In *Quodlibetalis* 3, Aquinas again explains his position on the obligation imposed by conscience, resuming and making more precise his argument from the Commentary. Every human act is sinful or meritorious in so far as it is voluntary. An act is specified by its object, not the material object, but the formal object. The formal object of the will is the good as apprehended and presented by the reason. Therefore, a human act is judged in its morality according to the good as apprehended, for this good moves the will. This rule is valid for all acts of the will, whether they are indifferent in themselves or whether they have an objective morality. Should the conscience command as forbidden by God the raising of a beam from the ground, and should one nevertheless raise the beam, his will *per se* and formally chooses an action which is contrary to the law, even though it may not be contrary materially. There is contempt of the law, and therefore sin. The Angelic Doctor concludes with the statement that conscience, whether true or erroneous, whether it commands indifferent or *per se* evil acts, obliges, so that one sins by disobeying the command.[47]

In the *Summa Theologica,* once again Thomas treats the question of the obligations of conscience. He entitles the first article in which he treats this subject, "Whether the will is evil when it is at variance with erring reason?", and in the body of the article, he states that this title means the same as asking "whether an erring conscience binds."[48] Thomas gives the traditional Franciscan opinion on this matter, basing obligation on the intrinsic morality of the act prescribed by conscience, and then he immediately rejects this position as unreasonable:

> In matters of indifference, the will that is at variance with erring reason or conscience, is evil in some way on account of the object, on which the goodness or malice of the will depends; not indeed on account of the object according as it is in its own nature, but according as it is accidentally apprehended by reason as something evil to do or to avoid . . . . From the very fact that a thing is proposed by the reason as being evil, the will, by tending thereto becomes evil. And this is the case not only in indifferent matters but also in those that are good or evil in themselves. For not only indifferent matters can receive the character of

goodness or malice accidentally, but also that which is good can receive the character of evil, or that which is evil can receive the character of goodness, on account of the reason apprehending it as such.[49]

Thus, Saint Thomas holds to his original position as stated in the *Commentary on the Sentences*. Every will at variance with reason, whether the reason be true or erroneous, is evil, or in other words, conscience binds, whether it is true or erroneous.

In a word, the teaching of Saint Thomas Aquinas on erroneous conscience can be summed up in this text:

Erroneous conscience binds even in things intrinsically evil. For conscience binds, as has been said, in this, that if someone acts contrary to his conscience, it follows that he has the will to sin. Thus if someone believes that to omit fornication is a mortal sin, when he chooses not to fornicate, he chooses to sin mortally, and therefore, sins mortally.[50]

In this text, Thomas summarizes his teaching on the obligations of conscience. He had stated his position in the *Commentary on the Sentences*, developed and explained it in subsequent works, and here, he summarizes it. In replying to the objection that to obey erroneous conscience is to act contrary to the law of God, Thomas puts the finishing touches, as it were, on his doctrine. He writes that the objection that the dictate of the erroneous conscience is contrary to the law of God is not a valid one, for the obligation of an erroneous conscience is the same as that of the law of God. Conscience does not dictate anything unless it believes it is in keeping with the law of God; this law is not applied to man except by means of his conscience.[51]

§4 ERRONEOUS CONSCIENCE AND IGNORANCE

This then is the teaching of the Angelic Doctor on the obligations imposed by conscience, but it is by no means his complete doctrine. A further question remains. What is the morality of following one's conscience when it is at variance with the law? In order to answer this question, and explain the related one referred to previously that one sins by disobeying his erroneous conscience and yet sins in following it, it is necessary to investigate the teaching of Aquinas on ignorance. The Angelic Doctor points this out himself when he writes that the solution to this question depends on what was taught about ignorance, since ignorance sometimes causes an act to be involuntary, and sometimes not, and moral goodness and evil consist in action in so far as it is voluntary.[52]

Saint Thomas teaches that sin is the same as *culpa*, and thus, every sin must be voluntary. He also reasons that sin is nothing else but an evil human act, and since a human act must be a voluntary one, it follows that to have sin, the act must be voluntary.[53] Therefore, anything what would lessen or take away the voluntariness of a human act would lessen or take away its sinfulness.[54] Now, applying this to conscience, it is seen that the dictates of conscience depend on the knowledge supplied by reason, and therefore, error in the conscience is a result of ignorance.[55] Certain types of ignorance lessen or take away voluntariness, and in these cases, a materially evil act performed in obedience to conscience would not be wholly imputable or would not be formally sinful.[56]

These types of ignorance which will excuse an act can be culled from various texts in Saint Thomas. He divides ignorance first into three categories. On the part of the agent, ignorance may be either vincible or invincible. Vincible ignorance, or that over which the agent has control, may arise either because the agent does not know what he can immediately know or because he causes the ignorance, as happens when a man willingly gets drunk. Invincible ignorance is that over which the agent has no control. On the part of the knowledge involved, there may be ignorance of that which one is obliged to know, and this is called ignorance of a universal, or ignorance of law; or there may be ignorance of something which one is not held to know, and this is ignorance of particular circumstances, or ignorance of fact. Saint Thomas draws his third division from the ordination which ignorance has to the act which follows. Some ignorance is the cause of the act, because if there were no ignorance, the act would not be performed. Other ignorance is not the cause of the act, e.g., one approaches a woman to commit fornication, believing she is a certain woman, but in reality, she is not that woman; yet, even if he knew she were different, he would still approach her.[57]

Using these distinctions, Aquinas states that ignorance excuses or lessens sin in so far as it causes involuntariness, for what is unknown cannot be voluntary. Ignorance which does not cause an act, does not cause involuntariness, and does not excuse. Ignorance which causes an act can excuse from sin either partially or totally; if the ignorance itself is totally without fault, then it excuses totally, e.g., invincible ignorance and ignorance of a particular fact, provided that diligence was used to try to overcome the ignorance. If the ignorance itself has some guilt connected with it, it excuses partially, since it causes some involuntariness, though it retains also a partial voluntariness. Thus, ignorance of a universal partially excuses; likewise vincible ignorance would excuse partially if a man did something illicit when he incurred the ignorance, and would excuse totally if he did something which was licit and this resulted in the ignorance.[58] Thus, as a general principle, Thomas establishes that in so far as ignorance is the cause of involuntariness, it excuses the subsequent act from sin. In his later works, he repeats, modifies, and re-explains this general principle and its treatment. Concerning ignorance as an excuse for a subsequent action, Aquinas teaches that if the ignorance causes involuntariness, it excuses; if the ignorance itself, however, is sinful, it does not excuse. Thus, he writes:

Ignorance which is the cause of an act, causes involuntariness; whence it always excuses, unless the ignorance itself is a sin. Ignorance is a sin when one is ignorant of what he can and should know.[59]

Ignorance can fall under the will, and become voluntary in three ways. First, when someone directly wills not to know the science of salvation, lest he be deterred from sin . . . . Secondly, ignorance may be indirectly voluntary, because someone does not study in order to know, and this is ignorance of negligence. But one is not called negligent unless he does not apply his mind to knowing what he should know . . . . Thirdly, ignorance may be voluntary accidentally, namely, when someone directly or indirectly wills something from which ignorance follows . . . as exemplified in one who is drunk, who willingly drank to excess (or) when someone neglects to repel a movement of rising passion.[60]

Ignorance has a threefold relationship to the act of the will . . . . Concomitantly, when there is ignorance of what is done; but so that even if it were known, it would be done . . . . Ignorance of this kind does not cause involuntariness, . . . since it is not the cause of anything that is repugnant to the will; but it causes non-voluntariness, since that which is unknown cannot be actually willed. Ignorance is consequent to the act of the will in so far as ignorance itself is voluntary . . . ; as when a man wishes not to know . . . and this is called affected ignorance. When it regards that which one can and ought to know, ignorance is also voluntary . . . . Ignorance of this kind happens either when one does not actually consider what he can and ought to consider, . . . or when one does not take the trouble to acquire the knowledge one ought to have, in which sense, ignorance of the general principles of law, which one ought to know, is voluntary.... If in either of these ways, ignorance is voluntary, it cannot cause involuntariness simply. Nevertheless, it causes involuntariness in a certain respect, in as much as it precedes the movement of the will toward the act, which movement would not take place if there were knowledge. Ignorance is antecedent to the act of the will when it is not voluntary, and yet it is the cause of the man's willing what he would not will otherwise.... Such ignorance causes involuntariness simply.[61]

Ignorance denotes a ... lack of knowledge of those things one has a natural aptitude to know. Some of those we are under obligation to know, those, to wit, without the knowledge of which we are unable to accomplish a due act rightly. Wherefore, we are all bound to know the articles of faith, and the universal principles of right, and each individual is bound to know matters regarding his duty or state. Now, there are other things which a man may have a natural aptitude to know, yet he is not bound to know them.... Ignorance of what one is bound to know is a sin, whereas it is not imputed as a sin to man if he fails to know what he is unable to know.... Consequently, ignorance of such thing is called invincible ignorance, because it cannot be overcome by study, (and) ... not being voluntary ... is not a sin; wherefore it is evident that no invincible ignorance is a sin. On the other hand, vincible ignorance is a sin, if it be about matters one is bound to know, but not if it be about things one is not bound to know.[62]

Ignorance which is not the cause of the sinful act ... since it does not make the act to be involuntary, does not excuse from sin. The same applies to any ignorance that does not cause, but follows or accompanies the sinful act. On the other hand, ignorance which is the cause of the act, since it makes it to be involuntary, of its very nature excuses from sin, because voluntariness is essential to sin. But it may fail to excuse altogether from sin: . . . it may happen that a person does not know some circumstance of a sin, the knowledge of which circumstance would prevent him from sinning . . . and nevertheless, his knowledge is sufficient for him to be aware that the act is sinful. . . . Or this may happen on the part of the ignorance itself, because this ignorance is voluntary, either directly, as when a man wishes of set purpose to be ignorant of certain things that he may sin more freely, or indirectly, as when a man, through stress of work or because of other occupations, neglects to acquire the knowledge which would restrain him from sin. Such negligence renders the ignorance itself voluntary and sinful, provided it be about matters one is bound and able to know. Consequently, this ignorance does not altogether excuse from sin. If, however, the ignorance be such as to be entirely involuntary, either through being invincible, or through being of matters one is not bound to know, then such ignorance excuses from sin altogether.[63]

Thus, it is easily seen that Saint Thomas teaches that if ignorance is involuntary in itself and causes involuntariness with regard to a subsequent act, the ignorance offers an excuse from sin. If the ignorance is voluntary and sinful itself, it does not excuse. And there is also a middle ground: if ignorance is only partial, it excuses in so far as it affects the subsequent action. One thing worthy of note is that Saint Thomas uses the terms vincible and invincible in a different sense from modern theologians. This appears to result from a slightly different definition of ignorance. The Angelic Doctor defines ignorance as the lack of knowledge of those things one has a natural aptitude to know, and he defines nescience as the simple absence of knowledge. With this in mind, Aquinas defines invincible ignorance as ignorance of those things which man is unable to know, which ignorance cannot be overcome by study. Vincible ignorance is that which can be overcome through study, and includes both what man is bound to know and what he is not bound to know, and thus a priest who does not know the geometric theorems is vincibly ignorant.[64] Thomas equates invincible ignorance and inculpability: "wherefore, it is evident that no invincible ignorance is a sin."[65] Vincible ignorance, according to Saint Thomas, may be either culpable or inculpable: "vincible ignorance is a sin, if it deals with something one is bound to know; but not if it concerns what one is not bound to know."[66]

Modern theologians define ignorance as used in moral theology as the privation of knowledge in a subject who should have it, and nescience as the simple lack of knowledge, whether the knowledge be due or not. Thus, invincible ignorance is that which cannot be overcome with moral diligence, and because of the definition of ignorance, those things which man is not bound to know are not included in this type of ignorance; rather they fall under nescience. Vincible ignorance is that which can be overcome, but is not because of negligence or ill will.[67] Though the terminology is the same in Thomas and in modern manuals, the concept is slightly different.

With regard to ignorance of fact, Thomas writes that it excuses; but concerning ignorance of law, Aquinas seems at first sight to contradict himself. He writes:

> Ignorance of law does not excuse, because it is a sin itself; ignorance of fact excuses.[68]

> Ignorance of law does not excuse from sin, unless it is invincible, in which case it totally excuses.[69]

> Ignorance . . . which is one's fault, excuses partially, namely, in so far as it is ignorance, because it thus causes involuntariness; but it does not excuse in so

far as it is one's fault, because in this case, it retains the nature of a voluntary; and therefore, ignorance of a universal (ignorance of law) excuses a subsequent sin not totally but partially.[70]

However, if these texts are taken in their contexts and together with the rest of the teaching of Aquinas on ignorance, it will be easily seen that there is no contradiction. When he wrote that ignorance of the law is a sin and therefore, did not excuse, the Angelic Doctor was referring to ignorance of a divine law which all can and should know.[71] Ignorance of this type is vincible and culpable in the scheme of Thomas, and therefore, is no excuse. The partial excuse offered by ignorance of law needs no further explanation, since the text above explains the reason. That ignorance of law excuses totally if it is invincible fits in well with the teaching of Aquinas. Since, as has been demonstrated above, no invincible ignorance is a sin, it is only logical that ignorance of law, if it is invincible, is not a sin. Thomas himself gives an example of such a case when he writes that all are bound to know a papal decree, but if someone cannot know such a decree, e.g., if he is in prison or in a foreign land in which the decree is not yet promulgated, then his ignorance excuses him from sin if he acts contrary to the decree.[72] Such ignorance is ignorance of law; yet it excuses. Father Bertke also notes that Saint Thomas admits that ignorance of law sometimes excuses:

> Texts in Saint Thomas might be quoted which apparently prove that he believed *ignorantia iuris* always contained at least some culpability. However, if we go to his *ex professo* treatment of ignorance, we find that . . . he holds that ignorance, considered in itself, and as the cause of the acts, constitutes an excuse from sin, for the consequent act is involuntary as a result of the previous ignorance. True, the ignorance itself may be voluntary and thus a sin, as in the case of *ignorantia affectata*. Another case in which ignorance itself may be a sin happens when one is

obliged to know a truth, but neglects to acquire the knowledge because of laziness. This is true only when the person is obliged to know the truth and *can* know the truth — *dummodo sit eroum quae quis scire tenetur et potest* (I-II, 76, 3, c).[73]

The doctrine of Saint Thomas concerning erroneous conscience is to be understood in the light of his teaching on ignorance. If the ignorance from which the error of conscience results causes the subsequent action to be involuntary, then the ignorance is an excuse from sin. Therefore, if one were to act out of invincible ignorance, or inculpably vincible ignorance, he would not sin in following an erroneous conscience.[74]

With this in mind, it is possible now to give a reply to the problem raised earlier in this chapter, i.e., if one obeys an erroneous conscience, he sins, and if he disobeys it, sin is committed.[75] Deman points out that both Lottin and DeBlic[76] speak of this problem and interpret the sayings of Thomas as a result of the moral objectivism of the times. They claim Thomas did not understand the subjective conditions of morality, and that the Angelic Doctor taught that to act contrary to the law was always sinful, even to the point that every material sin is a formal one. However, it is our opinion, in agreement with Deman, that this interpretation is indeed a strange one, considering the doctrine of Thomas on ignorance and the voluntary. When Thomas wrote that what is contrary to the law is evil, he understood this as the definition of moral evil. It is the role of conscience to be in conformity with the law; if it is not, then it falls under the definition of moral evil. But this does not exclude the possibility that when conscience does not conform to the law that the nonconformity is accidental. Saint Thomas himself wrote that when one adheres to an erroneous conscience, he does so because of the truth he believes to be present there; he adheres to a true conscience, which is false *quasi per accidens.*[77] Deman continues, quoting Saint Vincent Ferrer and backing up his position with the authority of Antoninus and Adrian VI:

> Those words of Saint Thomas: 'what is done contrary to the law . . . " must be understood with this exception: unless perhaps conscience errs invincibly and inculpably. . . . And this is only right; for it is the constant opinion of Thomas that an invincibly erroneous conscience excuses from sin.[78]

This interpretation of Deman seems to be the only logical interpretation possible of the problem. Considering what Aquinas wrote on ignorance and its effects on the voluntary, and also considering the dictum of Thomas that all sin is voluntary, it would be completely contradictory for the Angelic Doctor to write that one would commit a sin by following the dictates of an erroneous conscience if the error were caused by inculpable ignorance which rendered the action involuntary. The quotation from *Quodlibetalis* 8[79] should be understood, then, with the restriction that invincible or inculpable ignorance excuses from sin.[80] This argument is also strengthened when the question is seen in context:

> One can be obliged to sin from the part of conscience, whether he has certainty about the opposite of what he does, or whether he has opinion with some doubt. That which is done contrary to the law is always evil, nor is one excused because he acts according to his conscience.[81]

In context, Aquinas is speaking of one who is certain that the contrary of what conscience dictates is the right thing, or of one who has some doubt about the morality of his proposed action. In these cases, it would be sinful to follow the erroneous conscience.

§5 ERRONEOUS CONSCIENCE AND THE COMMAND OF A SUPERIOR

Another question to be discussed is that concerning conscience and the dictate of a superior. In chapter 2,[82] it was stated that Saint Bonaventure's statement that the precept of a superior binds more than the dictate of conscience was not opposed to the doctrine of Saint Thomas. The Angelic Doctor writes that the bond imposed by conscience is greater than that imposed by the precept of a superior, since conscience binds in virtue of a divine command. Saint Thomas distinguishes, however, the situation in which one's conscience is true from one in which it is erroneous. If there is a true conscience, it binds absolutely and perfectly against the command of a superior. One cannot be freed from the obligation imposed by a true conscience, nor does one sin in following it, even though there is a command of a superior to the contrary. It should be noted that Aquinas is speaking of the command of a superior to do or omit what is referred to as an indifferent act, i.e., one not included under the vows or the rule. On the other hand, if one has an erroneous conscience, it also binds contrary to the command of a superior, but only imperfectly. It binds only on the condition that it endures; and one sins in following such a conscience, for he disobeys the superior, and he sins in obeying the superior, for he acts contrary to his conscience.[83]

Taking this in the light of the whole doctrine of Aquinas on the obligation imposed by conscience, this last statement must be interpreted as referring to a vincibly and culpably erroneous conscience. If the conscience were invincibly erroneous, then it would be impossible to change it; one could not set it aside and thus the action would be involuntary, and not sinful. Were the conscience vincibly erroneous, then it could and must be set aside, and man could thus avoid sin. This is shown by Aquinas when he points out that when a man has the obligation to follow his conscience and an opposite obligation to obey his superior, the obligation of conscience is greater in one sense, since it is more intense, i.e., conscience obliges *vi praecepti divini*, but less in another sense, since it can be removed more easily.[84] Thus, since he is speaking of an obligation of conscience which can be removed, he is obviously referring to a vincibly erroneous conscience.

Now Bonaventure, in his statement, also refers to an erroneous conscience. He writes that the command of a superrior is to be preferred over conscience especially when the superior commands what he can and should command.[85] In context, the Franciscan is speaking of a man who is in a quandary because of contrary obligations. Since the superior is commanding what is in his power to command, it is the conscience of the subject which is in error; Bonaventure does not mention the case of the subject with a true conscience.[86] Therefore, this statement of Bonaventure must be compared with the teaching of Thomas only on erroneous conscience and the command of a superior. When this comparison is made, it is clear that there is only an apparent discrepancy, and that in the manner of expression. Aquinas says that the obligation of conscience is greater because it is more intense, but less since it can be more easily removed. In fact, one has an obligation to set aside such a conscience in order to avoid sin. Thus, practically speaking, it is the superior who is to be obeyed. This is what Saint Bonaventure also teaches. The Franciscan does not consider the obligation which exists while the conscience remains, but simply gives a practical norm.

Saint Bonaventure does not explicity speak of a superior who commands indifferent acts; however, he implies it by the use of the word "especially" in the text. Thus it seems legitimate to speculate about what Bonaventure would teach if indifferent matter were the object of the command of the superior. He taught that an indifferent thing becomes obligatory if commanded by conscience. One could then either perform the act or set aside the conscience, since the conscience is erroneous with an error that is not dangerous to salvation.[87] With such a conscience in the face of an opposite command of a superior about the same act, it seems logical to conclude that Bonaventure would hold that the conscience must be set aside in favor of the superior. Thus, again, practically speaking, the teaching of Bonaventure and Aquinas on this point would not be contrary, but would only appear so from the words used to state the doctrine.

§6 THE MORALITY OF AN ACT DONE IN OBEDIENCE TO AN ERRONEOUS CONSCIENCE

It has been shown that the Angelic Doctor taught that erroneous conscience obliges that its commands be obeyed. If the ignorance which results in the erroneous conscience does not cause a subsequent evil action to be involuntary, the action is sinful; if the ignorance is the cause of involuntariness, the agent is excused from sin. This raises a final question: the agent is excused from sin, but is the action he performs morally good, and if the agent is in the state of grace, does he receive merit for this action, performed in good faith, following his invincibly erroneous conscience? Theologians since Saint Thomas are divided in this matter. Some claim that Thomas says that there is simply an excuse from sin, but no merit or goodness in the action; others interpret Aquinas as saying there is merit to be gained in following the dictates of an invincibly erroneous conscience.

Using Dom Lottin as a spokesman for those denying moral goodness or merit to an act done in conformity with an erroneous conscience, the arguments of these theologians and their interpretations of Saint Thomas can be indicated. In his discussion of the obligation of erroneous conscience, Lottin writes that, according to Saint Thomas, both true and false conscience oblige in the sense that one sins in not following them. Then he asks if one does morally good in following an erroneous conscience. Basing himself on the text, "if anyone does what is intrinsically evil, which erring reason judges good, sin is not avoided; if he does not do it, sin is incurred,"[88] Lottin writes that Aquinas agrees with the theological thought of the thirteenth century, denying moral goodness to an act done in obedience to an erroneous conscience. The reason is because it is not sufficient for an act to be morally good that it be apprehended as good, but that it also be objectively good.[89] Thus, Lottin interprets Thomas as denying moral goodness to such acts as are placed with erroneous conscience.[90] This is the application by Saint Thomas of the well-known axiom: *bonum ex integra causa, malum ex quocumque defectu*. As long as the error lasts, one commits sin whether he obeys his conscience or not. This is not to leave a man in a quandary, for he can set aside the erroneous conscience, and thus, act without sin.[91] Lottin goes on to note that Saint Thomas refused to draw the conclusion that an act done in conformity with an erroneous conscience is morally good. He simply said such an act is excused from sin, even in his later works when he had integrated his solution with the general questions relative to ignorance.[92]

Commenting on the statement made by Saint Thomas in the *De Veritate* that erroneous conscience is not said to oblige in the sense that one does good in following it, but rather in the sense that one sins in not folloing it,[93] Lottin writes that this evidently shows that Aquinas teaches that one does not do a morally good work if he obeys his erroneous conscience. One is under obligation to set aside the error, for as long as the conscience remains, it binds under pain of sin. But to follow it would also be wrong.[94]

The problem reaches its zenith for Lottin in his commentary on the text from the *Summa Theologica*, I-II, q. 19, a.6. Lottin notes that this text poses a delicate problem; he also admits that Aquinas does not admit indifferent acts *in concreto*. In previous works, Thomas had said that even evil acts done in conformity with an erroneous conscience are excused from sin. If this is true, and there are no indifferent acts *in concreto*, then hesitation does not seem possible in saying such acts must be good. But Lottin claims that Thomas does not hold this, as is evidenced by the text from the *Summa*. The article is entitled, "Whether the will is good when it abides by erring reason?".[95] In spite of this title, the solution to the question is simply that some ignorance excuses from fault. Lottin claims the title is phrased as it is simply to show an antithesis to article 5, entitled, "Whether the will is evil when it is at variance with erring reason?"[96] He also points out in favor of his argument that Thomas could easily have said an act done in accordance with erroneous conscience is good, but he did not; he simply replied that certain types of ignorance excuse from moral fault. The structure of article 6 is also cited as a proof for Lottin's position. Usually, the objections raised by Thomas indicate a position he does not hold, and they are corrected in the replies. In this article, each objection states that the will is good when it abides by erring reason, and this is an indication that Saint Thomas did not hold that position. Thomas simply wanted to show that one commits a moral fault by not following his conscience, even though it be erroneous; he did not want to canonize the act done in accordance with such a conscience.[97]

This seems to compromise the position of Saint Thomas, since he teaches one *must* obey an erroneous conscience. This is explained by Lottin in this manner. The subjective norm of conscience is sufficient to judge the moral evil of an action; but an act is morally good only if it conforms both to the dictates of conscience and to the demands of objective morality. The reason for this is the axiom: *bonum ex integra causa, malum ex quocumque defectu*. But this answer raises yet another question: by what right is the violation of a law which is not known imputable? This can be answered by investigating what knowledge is necessary and sufficient, in the mind of Aquinas, in order that the objective morality may be imputed to the agent. Dom Lottin answers:

When dealing with the circumstances of an action and presupposing that one can know these circumstances, ordinarily one should not make inquiries about them; ignorance regarding them (*ignorantia facti*) is in no way culpable; the subsequent act is consequently untainted by any moral guilt. But one would have to reason quite differently if this ignorance is directed toward the objective moral malice of an act (*ignorantia iuris*). Undoubtedly, it happens that one could know of the latter: (Saint Thomas foresaw these cases of impossibility or of invincible ignorance; they obviously excuse from all guilt). But supposing that we could have this knowledge of the objective order, we should acquire it; here, the one who could, should. Even an actual advertence to this obligation of overcoming the ignorance would not be required in order to render this ignorance culpable; the advertence, which ancient authors called interpretative, would suffice here to produce moral disorder; we do not say a complete moral disorder which implies serious sin, but an imperfect disorder which Saint Thomas calls venial sin.

We are then in a position to respond to this last point which could be made. Since, according to Saint Thomas, there are no individual indifferent acts, from the fact that an act evil in itself erroneously appears to be morally good, he cannot be satisfied with excusing it from guilt, he ought to declare it formally good.

Saint Thomas makes a straightforward answer in this sixth article: error of conscience can spring from an ignorance of principles directed toward the objective malice of the act considered *in abstracto;* in this case the act resulting from the error, far from being formally good, is formally evil, because excepting the case of a physical impossibility of inquiring into the moral law, this act proceeds from a voluntary *ignorantia consequens* of something which one is obliged to know. In this regard, it makes little difference that the act be related to a good end; as will be seen later, the pursuit of a praiseworthy end does not suffice to render an evil act good; the act of a person who lies to save his friend is and remains evil despite the nobility of the end he endeavors to obtain.

But a second case can occur: error coming from ignorance of detail, dealing with the circumstances of a concrete act which one could not or would not have to know; the act resulting from this error can then be neither good nor evil. In fact this act proceeds from an antecedent involuntary ignorance of something which one would not have to know; but the antecedent ignorance removes entirely the note of voluntariness and consequently all formal morality from the act which proceeds from it. It would be a vain attempt to force Saint Thomas into making any pronouncement on the morality of such an act. The Angelic Doctor has every right to refuse taking any such position. It is only in regard to deliberate acts that he has declared any moral indifference impossible. However, the act is not deliberate from a moral point of view in as much as it proceeds from an antecedent ignorance of fact, neither as it appears in itself, nor in its cause, since the error is involuntary and innocent. Without a doubt, this concrete act could be related to an end and because of this end it would be deliberate; and it must be added that if this end is good, there is nothing here which restrict the goodness of the end from influencing the act itself, since the act not being evil, there is nothing on the part of the act itself placing an obstacle to this influence. The act will be good because it will be ultimately orientated toward a morally good end; but this act in as much as it proceeds from antecedent ignorance, is neither good nor evil; it is completely outside the order of formal morality, because its essential element, namely deliberation, is absent.[98]

This statement is self-explanatory. An act which is morally evil in itself can never be, of itself, a morally good act. If an erroneous conscience dictates such an act, and the error of conscience results from ignorance of fact, the act itself has no morality, since it is not a voluntary act; but taken together with the good intention of the agent, the concrete act is voluntary, and it receives its morality from the intention, becoming a good act. On the other hand, if the ignorance resulting in the erroneous conscience is ignorance of some principle bearing on the objective malice of an act considered in the abstract, then the act dictated by conscience is in itself formally evil. The reason is because it proceeds from consequent and voluntary ignorance of something that should be known.

This explanation of the mind of Saint Thomas is held by Lottin in common with other theologians,[99] the most vociferous of whom is D. Concina, an eighteenth century Dominican. He writes that lies, thefts, and other intrinsically evil actions are always evil, even though they may be represented as good; however, they are not imputed to the agent if they are performed through invincible ignorance. His explanation of this differs in word from that of Lottin. Concina writes that though there are no indifferent actions which proceed from deliberate reason, there are indifferent acts which proceed from necessity.[100]

Prümmer speaks of the controversy and gives a quotation from Concina in which the latter speaks with calculated vehemence against those who do not hold his position. Prümmer writes:

>He (Concina) proclaims it an intolerable absurdity that someone can gain eternal life by performing an

evil action, e.g., idolatry, out of invincible ignorance. He says, 'What is more repugnant to common sense than that terrbile and horrid evils are transformed by a wondrous metamorphosis into virtues, into merit for eternal life? By what power? Divine? Never! By what power then? Hear and be stupefied: by the power of human error! The error of our mind is then another God.'[101]

As far as the problem itself is concerned, Prümmer is content to give a short summary of both sides of the controversy without explicitly choosing between them. He does note that the position of Concina is adopted by only a few, and that it is not to be spurned. The opposite opinion is held by Saint Alphonsus, Beaudoin, Müller, and many modern theologians. He also notes that Saint Alphonsus refers to his own position as *probabilior et communissima*.[102]

Besides the theologians mentioned by Prümmer, there are two whose opinion on the problem of merit and erroneous conscience deserve attention. C. LaCroix was a contemporary of Concina, and it seems to be against him that Concina wrote. LaCroix defended the position as *communissima* that one can and does gain merit by following an invincibly erroneous conscience. He writes that Saint Thomas taught that every human act in the concrete is good or evil, that an act done out of invincible ignorance is not evil (as even the adversaries of his position agree); therefore, it must be good.[103]

Taking up the problem in modern times, A. D. Sertillanges rallies to the support of LaCroix and those holding the more common position. He first recalls to mind some of the basic tenets of the Thomistic doctrine on erroneous conscience. Conscience obliges, i.e., it imposes necessity; this necessity is conditional, i.e., if one desires a reward, he must obey his conscience; the imposition of this necessity is through the contact of knowledge. Therefore, no one is bound unless he knows. He who is incapable of knowledge is incapable of obligation, and one who is ignorant is not bound unless he is obliged not to be ignorant.[104]

The Dominican then proceeds to set aside an objection often raised by those who deny the possibility of merit. He writes that if one does merit in performing an evil action through an erroneous conscience, it is not correct to say that it is the evil action which is meritorious; what is meritorious is the right intention, which, in this case, is represented by the evil action.[105]

Then, attacking the problem itself, Sertillanges points out that it is only natural to judge from the use of the axiom *bonum ex integra causa* . . . by Saint Thomas that an objectively evil action could not become meritorious. However, this seems to contradict the teaching of Aquinas that one must follow an invincibly erroneous conscience. Therefore, the teaching of the Angelic Doctor on this point must be interpreted harmoniously with his whole doctrine. If there is an error present, one must investigate to determine whether the error is imputable. If the will is evil, the action will not be good. If the contrary is true, nothing stands in the way of the act's being good, for the error, not being malicious or due to negligence, becomes the cause of an invincible deviation, and we cannot be blamed for something which is not our fault. One must conclude then, that an act evil in itself, but which one believes to be good through the dictates of an invincibly erroneous conscience, is virtuous and meritorius, if one is to be consistent in following the principles of Saint Thomas. Nothing justifies the half-measure of claiming such an act is simply excused. Conscience represents the law for us, and to follow one's conscience is to follow the law formally, even though it may happen that one does not follow the law materially.[106]

Summing up his position in this matter, Sertillanges writes:

> Good in itself is a rule in itself. Supposing the will be be well ordered, what appears good to us is a rule for us. Things must not be confused, and one should not declare that a good in itself is, by that very fact, here and now, a rule for us, nor that what appears good to us becomes, by that fact, a good in itself. When I behold something which appears good to me, in so far as I am a voluntary agent, I am qualified by that good, although the objectivity of the case may be otherwise. Even if I have not followed *the* law, I was able to follow *my* law, and, as a moral subject, I was able to act in accordance with law. To speak thus is not to render morality subjective, but only to speak of the morality of the subject, which is only natural.[107]

We can now pass to a consideration of the texts from Saint Thomas which are used in this question. In stating the position of Lottin,[108] the interpretations of those denying merit were pointed out; but there are other possible interpretations. L. Frins demonstrates this when he defends the position of Sertillanges, stated above. In the *Summa Theologica,* Saint Thomas asks whether the will is good when it abides by erring reason. Immediately, in beginning his reply, he notes that this is the same as to ask whether an erroneous conscience excuses.[109] Therefore, it is the same thing to say that an invincibly erroneous conscience excuses (which Thomas does conclude and which those holding the opposite position concede) as to say that the will abiding by that conscience is good. Thomas does not deny this assertion; in fact, it follows most logically from his whole doctrine. He denies the existence of indifferent acts *in concreto,*[110] and thus, if an act is not evil, it must be good. In the previous article, Aquinas writes that that which is evil can receive the *rationem boni* because of the reason apprehending it as good.[111] From the whole doctrine of Thomas as presented in this chapter, it is evident that this refers only to invincible and inculpable ignorance which causes the reason to apprehend an evil as good. If the ignorance were vincible and culpable, then the agent would sin in following the conscience; he would be bound to set it aside.

In the *De Veritate,* q. 17, a.4, Thomas writes that erroneous conscience obliges not in the sense that one always does right in obeying it, but rather in the sense that one sins in not following it. This is interpreted in this manner. As long as the conscience remains, one sins in not obeying its dictates; but it is not *always* true one does good by obeying such a conscience. If the conscience is erroneous because of one's own fault, if it is vincibly and culpably erroneous, then it is sinful to obey the conscience. But it does not follow that one sins in following an invincibly erroneous conscience. Saint Thomas says one does not *always* do right in following erroneous conscience; thus, *sometimes,* he may do right. In the light of the whole doctrine of Aquinas, one would do right in following an invincibly erroneous conscience.

Another text used is taken from *II Sent.,* d. 39, q. 3, ad 3, where Thomas writes that one sins in doing something intrinsically evil which erring conscience judges to be good, and if it is not done, sin is also committed. Here, Aquinas is referring to a vincibly erroneous conscience, not to one which is invincibly erroneous. This is shown by the fact that in response to the fifth objection, Thomas speaks of an erroneous conscience which must be set aside, which is true only of one which is vincibly erroneous. Similarly, in the article itself, he points out that if a man does something evil which he thinks is good, sin is not avoided. This is true only if the conscience is vincibly erroneous, since it is explicitly stated in the article referred to above from the *Summa* that an invincibly erroneous conscience excuses from sin.

The final text which is quoted in this controversy is taken from *Quodlibetalis* 8, a. 13: whatever is done contrary to the law is always evil, nor is it excused by the fact that it is done in accordance with conscience. The interpretation of this text is the same as the preceding one: if it is done in accordance with a vincibly erroneous conscience, the act is formally evil; if it is done through an invincibly erroneous conscience, the act is only materially evil.[112]

The position which holds that an evil act done in accordance with the dictates of an invincibly erroneous conscience is morally good and even meritorious is more logical and more in keeping with the whole doctrine of Saint Thomas on conscience, while the opposite opinion seems to do injustice to some tenets of the Angelic Doctor. It is true that there are some texts, which, if taken by themselves, seem to indicate that Saint Thomas favored the negative opinion, but when taken in context and viewed in the light of the general teaching of Aquinas, they fit neatly into place. It is for these reasons that our position in this matter is in agreement with Frins and Sertillanges:[113] one who follows the dictates of an invincibly erroneous conscience and thereby does an act which is objectively evil is, according to Aquinas, obeying the law of God formally and does not sin; rather the act, as a whole, is morally good, and if the other conditions necessary for merit are present, merit is gained. It is not without reason that Thomas writes:

> Although an act is specified by its object, it is not specified by it according to the *materiam objecti,* but rather according to the *rationem objecti.* . . . Every human act is sinful or meritorious, in so far as it is voluntary; now the object of the will is good as apprehended, and therefore, a human act is judged virtuous or vicious according to the good as apprehended toward which the will is drawn, and not according to the material object of the act.[114]

FOOTNOTES

1. This work is dated by authorities as being written between 1254 and 1256. See Copleston, F., S. J., *A History of Philosophy 2* (Newman Press, Westminster, Md., 1955) 304; Gilson, E., *The Christian Philosophy of Saint Thomas Aquinas* (Random House, New York, 1956) in the appendix by I. T. Eschmann, O. P., 384. See also Walz, P. A., "Thomas d'Aquin (saint), Ecrits," *DTC* 15.1 (1946) 637-41, where he uses many authorities to date the works of Saint Thomas. He also notes that Pelster dates the work between 1253 and 1255; this however, is still in agreement that the Commentary is the first of Thomas's works dealing with this question.

2. Both Thomas and Bonaventure died in 1274.

3. See *In II Sent.*, d. 24, q. 2, a. 4, sol. (ed. Vivès, *Opera Omnia*, 8, 1873) 320.

4. See chapter 1, p. 3.

5. Nullo autem horum modorum conscientia sumitur secundum quod in usum loquentium venit, prout dicitur ligare vel aggravare peccatum: nullus enim ligatur ad aliquid faciendum nisi per hoc quod considerat hoc esse agendum; unde quamdam actualem considerationem rationis per conscientiam, communiter loquentes intelligere videntur. *In II Sent., loc. cit.*

6. See chapter 3, pp. 45-6; Lottin, *Psychologie et morale*, 228.

7. Ratio in eligendis et fugiendis, quisbusdam syllogismis utitur. In syllogismis autem est triplex consideratio, secundum tres propositiones, ex quarum duabus tertia concluditur. Ita etiam contingit in proposito, dum ratio in operandis ex universalibus principiis circa particularia judicium assumit. Et quia universalia principia iuris ad synderesim pertinent, rationes autem magis appropriate ad opus pertinent ad habitus, quibus ratio superior et inferior distinguuntur; synderesis in hoc syllogismo quasi majorem ministrat, cujus consideratio est actus synderesis; sed minorem ministrat ratio superior vel inferior, et eius consideratio est ipsius actus; sed consideratio conclusionis elicitae est consideratio conscientiae. *In II Sent., loc. cit.*

8. This is what theologians today call consequent and antecedent conscience. See Prümmer, *Manuale*, 199; Regatillo-Zalba, *Summa*, 245; Aertnys, J.,—Damen, C., C. SS. R., *Theologia Moralis* 1 (ed. 16, Marietti, Rome, 1950) 63.

9. See *In II Sent.*, *loc. cit.*

10. Lex naturalis nominat ipsa universalia principia iuris, synderesis vero nominat habitum eorum, seu potentia cum habitu; conscientia vero nominat applicationem quamdam legis naturalis ad aliquid faciendum per modum conclusionis cujusdam.—*loc. cit.*

11. See *ibid.*, ad 2, 321.

12. See *ibid.*, d. 39, q. 3, a.2, ad 3, 523.

13. See Walz, *loc. cit.;* Gilson, *op. cit.*, 390-91; Copleston, *loc. cit.*

14. La question *De Veritate* apporte quelque développements. La langage courant, norme de précision en matière de terminologie, servira de point de départ. La langue usuelle emploie indifferément certains mots, tel le mot *intellectus,* pour désigner à la fois l'acte, la puissance dont l'acte émane, et la disposition habituelle qui incline vers cet acte. . . . Au contraire, elle n'emploie le vocable *conscientia* que pour désigner l'acte de conscience. Pourquoi cette difference? Le même mot s'applique à l'acte et à la faculté dont il émane quant l'acte est propre à cette faculté; ainsi en est-il des mots *intellctus, visus.* Mais il arrive que l'acte convienne indifferément à plusieurs facultés; tel l'acte par lequel la faculté est appliquée à l'action, *usus;* . . . Ce, qui vient d'être dit du mot *usus* s'applique au mot *conscientia.* Car le mot "conscience" . . . n'implique aucune faculté, ni aucun habitus spécial de science dont la conscience serait l'acte propre. La "science", en effet, . . . est *quaecumque notitia.*—Lottin, O., "Les éléments de la moralité des actes chez S. Thomas d'Aquin," *RNS* 24 (1922) 411-12.

15. See Merkelbach, B. H., O. P. *Summa Theologiae Moralis I* (Desclee, Tournai, 1949) 187; Lottin, *Psychologie et morale,* 233.

16. See *De Veritate,* q. 17, a.1, resp. (*Opera Omnia,* ed. Vivès, 15, 1875) 70-71.

17. See *ibid.*, ad 9.

18. Applicatione qua consiliamur quid agendum sit, vel examinamus iam facta, applicantur ad actum habitus rationis operativi, scilicet habitus synderesis et habitus sapientiae, quo perficitur superior ratio, et habitus scientiae quo perficitur ratio inferior; sive simul omnes applicantur, sive alter eorum tantum. Ad hos enim habitus examinamus quae fecimus, et secundum eos consiliamur de faciendis.—*ibid.*, resp. Translation is from McGlynn, J. V., S. J., *Truth,* 2 (Regnery, Chicago, 1953) 319.

19. See Walz, *loc. cit.;* Gilson, *op. cit.,* 386-7; Copleston, *op. cit.,* 305.

20. Conscire . . . alterutrum dicat, aut habere socium in sciendo . . . aut ipsam scientiam terminari non ad unum obiectum, sed ad alterum quoque eo extendi.—Frins, V., S. J., *De Actibus Humanis* 3 (Herder, Fribourg in Brisgovia, 1911) 59.

21. See *Summa Theologica,* I, q. 79, a. 13, c. (ed. Leon, Rome, 5, 1889) 280-81.

22. See Rodrigo, L., S. J., *Praelectiones Theologico-Morales Comillenses* 3.1 (ed. Sal Terrae, Santander, 1954) 16-17.

23. See above, p. 70.

24. See *De Veritate,* q. 17, a. 2, resp. 73.

25. See *In II Sent.,* d. 39, q. 3, a. 2, 522-2; *De Veritate, loc. cit.; Quodl,* 3, q. 12, a. 26 (*Opera Omnia,* ed. Vivès, 15, 1875) 426.

26. In conclusione particularis agendi dupliciter contingit esse defectum. Uno modo ex falsitate principiorum ex quibus syllogizatur; et hoc modo in conclusione tenetur id quod veritati contrarium est: et hoc est error conscientiae. Alio modo ex impetu passionum absorbentium et quasi ligrantium rationis judicium in particulari ut actu non consideret nec hoc nec eius oppositum, sed voluntas sequatur delectabile quod sensus proponit; et hoc est error electionis et non conscientiae.—*In II Sent., loc. cit.*

27. Si diligenter videatur quomodo conscientia ligat, invenitur in omnibus ligare, ut alia opinio dicit. Conscientia enim quoddam dictamen rations est. Voluntas autem non movetur in aliquid appetendum, nisi praesupposita aliqua apprehensione; obiectum enim voluntatis est bonum vel malum, secundum quod est imaginatum vel intellectum. . . . Cum actus voluntatis ex obiecto specificatur, oportet quod secundum rationis iudicium et conscientiae, sit voluntatis actus, et per modum istum conscientia ligare dicitur: quia scilicet si aliquis fugiat per voluntatem quod ratio bonum dictat, est ibi fuga boni quae fuga malum est; quia voluntas fugit illud ac si esset bonum secundum rationem . . . et similiter si ratio dictat aliquod bonum esse malum, voluntas non potest in illud tendere, quin mala sit; tendit enim in illud ut ostensum est a ratione, . . . et ideo sive ratio sive conscientia recte judicet, sive non, voluntas obligatur hoc modo, quod si judicium vel dictamen rationis, quod est conscientia, non sequitur actus voluntatis, inordinatus est, et hoc est obligare, scilicet astringere voluntatem, ut non possit sine deformitatis nocumento in aliud tendere.—*In II Sent.,* d. 39, q. 3, a. 3 sol., 524.

28. See Lottin, "La valeur normative," 429.
29. *In II Sent.*, *loc. cit.*
30. Si fiat aliquid quod est secundum se malum, quod errans ratio judicat bonum, peccatum non evitatur; si autem non fiat, peccatum incurritur; quia unus defectus bonitatis sufficit ad hoc quod aliquid dicatur malum, sive desit bonitas quae est per accidens, secundum quod res apprehenditur in ratione boni, sive bonitas quae est rei per se; sed si altera sit tantum, scilicet quae est per accidens, non propter hoc erit actus bonus.—*loc. cit.*
31. See *ibid.*, ad 5.
32. See *ibid.*, ad 3.
33. See *De Veritate*, q. 17, a. 3, resp., 74-5.
34. This also gives us an insight into what Thomas meant when he wrote that conscience obliges in virtue of a divine precept: one sins by not obeying his conscience; therefore, the precept in question must be that conscience must be obeyed. In later works, as shall be seen in the development of this chapter, Thomas makes this more explicit.
35. See *De Veritate*, q. 17, a. 4, resp., 77.
36. Non autem videtur possibile quod aliquis peccatum evadat, si conscientia, quantumcumque errans, dictet aliquod esse praeceptum Dei quod sit indifferens sive per se malum, si contrarium, tali conscientia manente, agere disponat. Quantum enim in se est, ex hoc ipso habet voluntatem legem Dei non observandi unde mortaliter peccat. Quamvis igitur talis conscientia, quae est erronea, deponi possit; nihilominus tamen, dum manet, obligatoria est; quia transgressor ipsius de necessitate peccatum incurrit. — *loc. cit.* Translation is from McGlynn, *Truth*, 332.
37. See above, p. 75.
38. See *De Veritate*, *loc. cit.*
39. See *loc. cit.*
40. See Walz, "Thomas d'aquin, Ecrits," 639-40.
41. See Walz, *loc. cit.*; Gilson, *The Christian Philosophy* 386-7.
42. Walz, *loc. cit.*; Gilson, *op. cit.*, 392.
43. See Gilson, *loc. cit.*
44. See Walz, *loc. cit.*

45. See above, p. 75.

46. Illud autem quod agitur contra legem, semper est malum; nec excusatur per hoc quod est secundum conscientiam; et similiter quod est contra conscientiam est malum, quamvis non sit contra legem.—*Quodl*, 8, q. 6, a. 13 (*Opera Omnia*, ed. Vivès, 15, 1875) 540.

47. See *Quodl*, 3, q. 12, a. 27, resp. 426-7.

48. Utrum voluntas discordans a ratione errante sit mala . . . idem est . . . quod quaerere utrum conscientia errans obliget.—*Summa Theologica*, I-II, q. 19, a. 5, (ed. Leon., Rome, 6, 1891) 145. Translation is from Fathers of the English Dominican Province, *Summa Theologica of Saint Thomas Aquinas* 1 (Benziger, New York, 1947) 674. Hereafter, this work will be referred to as English Translation.

49. Sed hoc irrationabiliter dicitur. In indifferentibus enim, voluntas discordans a ratione vel conscientia errante, est mala aliquomodo propter obiectum, a quo bonitas vel malitia voluntatis dependet; non autem propter obiectum secundum sui naturam; sed secundum quod per accidens a ratione apprehenditur ut malum ad faciendum vel ad vitandum. . . . Ex eo quod aliquid proponitur a ratione ut malum, voluntas, dum in illud fertur, accipit rationem mali. Hoc autem contingit non solum in indifferentibus sed etiam in per se bonis vel malis. Non solum enim id quod est indifferens, potest accipere rationem boni vel mali per accidens; sed etiam id quod est bonum potest accipere rationem mali, vel illud quod est malum, rationem boni, propter apprehensionem rationis.—*loc. cit.*; trans: *loc. cit.*

50. Etiam in per se malis conscientia erronea ligat. Intantum enim conscientia ligat, ut dictum est, in quantum, ex hoc quod aliquis contra conscientiam agit, sequitur quod habet voluntatem peccandi, et ita si aliquis credat non fornicari esse peccatum mortale, dum elegit non fornicari, elegit peccare mortaliter, et ita mortaliter peccat.—*In Epistolam ad Romanos*, c. 14, 1. 2 (*Opera Omnia*, ed. Vivès, 20, 1876) 580.

51. See *ibid*.

52. See *Summa Theologica*, I-II, q. 19, a. 6, resp., 146.

53. See *In II Sent.*, d. 41, q. 2, a. 1, 545; *Summa Theologica*, I-II, q. 71, a. 6, c. (ed. Leon., 7, 1892) 9.

54. See *Summa Theologica*, I-II, q. 76, a. 4, c., 57.

55. See *Quodl.* 8, q. 6, a. 15, 542.

56. See *In II Sent.*, d. 22, q. 2, sol., 292-3; *De Malo*, q. 3, a. 8 (*Opera Omnia*, ed. Vivès, 13, 1875) 394-5; *Summa Theologica*, I-II, q. 76, a. 3, c., 55.

What is said here about ignorance also applies in some way to inadvertence, since ignorance is a habitual privation of knowledge, and inadvertence is an actual privation, i.e., non-consideration of knowledge which is in fact present. In the *Summa Theologica*, I-II, 77, 2, c., Thomas writes that it can happen that one does not consider actually that which is known habitually, so that a man who has correct knowledge does not consider this knowledge and thus a man can act counter to what he knows but does not actually consider. This is inadvertence, and may happen because of lack of attention or because of some supervening hindrance.

Now, ignorance of what one can and should know can be considered as actual or habitual. If it is habitual, then the ignorance is culpable and does not entirely excuse, though in so far as it is ignorance, it lessens the voluntary (see pp.   ). If the ignorance is actual, then it is inadvertence; if it is culpable and deliberately willed, it does not excuse; if it is culpable, but not deliberately willed here and now, as happens when one is vincibly ignorant but does not advert to that fact here and now, then one is guilty in cause. However, if one is culpably ignorant and then tries to overcome his ignorance but cannot, inadvertence would excuse him; but if he adverted to his ignorance and nevertheless acted, he would not be excused unless the ignorance were rendered invincible.

57. See *In II Sent.*, *loc. cit.*

58. See *loc. cit.*

59. Ignorantia quae est causa actus causat involuntarium; unde semper excusat, nisi ipsa ignorantia sit peccatum. Est autem ignorantia peccatum, quando ignorat quis quae potest scire et tenetur.—*Quodl.* 1, q. 9, a. 19, resp., 374-5.

60. Ignorantia sub voluntate cadit, et fit voluntarie. Hoc autem fit tripliciter. Primo quidem quando aliquis directe vult ignorare scientiam salutis, ne retrahatur a peccato. . . . Secundo, ignorantia dicitur voluntaria indirecte, quia non adhibet studium ad cognoscendum, et hic est ignorantia negligentiae. Sed . . . non dicitur aliquis negligere nisi . . . non applicet animum ad cognoscendum ea quae cognoscere debet. . . . Tertio dicitur aliqua ignorantia

voluntaria per accidens, ex eo scilicet, quod aliquis directe vel indirecte vult aliquid ad quod sequitur ipsum ignorare . . . sicut apparet in ebrio, qui vult superflue vinum potare (vel) cum aliquis negligit repellere insurgentis passionis motus.—*De Malo*, q. 3, a. 8, resp., 394.

61. Sciendum est quod ignorantia tripliciter se habet ad actum voluntatis. . . . Concomitanter quidem quando ignorantia est de eo quod agitur, tamen etiam si sciretur, nihilominus ageretur. . . . Talis ignorantia non facit involuntarium' . . . quia non causat aliquid quod sit repugnans voluntati; sed facit non-voluntarium, quia non potest esse actu volitum quod ignoratum est. Consequenter autem se habet ignorantia ad voluntatem, in quantum ipsa ignorantia est voluntaria . . . sicut cum aliquis ignorare vult . . . et haec dicitur ignorantia affectata; alio modo dicitur voluntaria ignorantia eius quod quis potest scire et debet. . . . Hoc igitur modo dicitur ignorantia sive cum aliquis actu non considerat quod considerare potest et debet, . . . sive cum aliquis notitiam quam debet habere, non curat acquirere, et secundum hunc modum ignorantia universalis iuris, quae quis scire tenetur, voluntaria dicitur. . . . Cum autem ipsa ignorantia sit voluntaria aliquo istorum modorum, non potes causare simpliciter involuntarium; causat tamen secundum quid involuntarium in quantum praecedit motum voluntatis ad aliquid agendum, qui non esset, scientia praesente. Antecendenter autem se habet ad voluntatem ignorantia quando non est voluntaria, et tamen est causa volendi quod alias homo non vellet. . . . Et talis ignorantia causat involuntarium simpliciter. — *Summa Theologica*, I-II, q. 6, a. 8, c., 62-3; Trans.:*English Translation* 1, 622.

62. Ignorantia vero importat scientiae privationem, dum scilicet deest scientia eorum quae aptus natus est scire. Horum autem quaedam aliquis scire tenetur: illa scilicet sine quorum scientia non potest debitum actum recte exercere. Unde omnes tenentur scire communiter ea quae sunt fidei, et universalia iuris praecepta: singuli autem ea quae ad eorum statum vel officium spectant. Quaedam vero sunt quae etsi aliquis natus est scire, non tamen ea scire tenetur. . . . Ignorantia eorum quae aliquis scire tenetur, est peccatum. Non autem imputatur homini ad negligentiam, si nesciat ea quae scire non potest. Unde horum ignorantia invincibilis dicitur: quia scilicet studio superari non potest. Et . . . cum non sit voluntaria, . . . non est peccatum. Ex quo patet quod nulla ignorantia invincibilis est peccatum: ignorantia autem vincibilis est peccatum, si sit eorum quae aliquis scire tenetur; non autem si sit eorum quae quis scire non tenetur.—*Summa Theologica*, I-II, q. 76, a. 2, c., 53 trans.: *English Translation*, 931.

63. Ignorantia, quae non est causa actus peccati . . . quia non causat involuntarium, non excusat a peccato. Et eadem ratio est de quacumque ignorantia non causante, sed consequente vel concomitante actum peccati. Sed ignorantia quae est causa actus, quia causat involuntarium, de se habet quod excuset a peccato: eo quod voluntarium est de ratione peccati. Sed quod aliquando non totaliter excuset a peccato: . . . potest contingere quod aliquis ignoret quidem aliquam circumstantiam peccati, quam si sciret, retraheretur a peccando, . . . et tamen adhuc remanet in eius scientia aliquid per quod cognoscit illud ess actum peccati. . . . Alio modo potest hoc contingere ex parte ipsius ignorantiae, quia scilicet ipsa ignorantia est voluntaria: vel directe, sicut cum aliquis studiose vult nescire aliqua, ut liberius peccet; vel indirecte, sicut cum aliquis propter laborem, vel propter alias occupationes, negligit addiscere id per quod a peccato retraheretur. Talis enim negligentia facit ignorantiam ipsam esse voluntariam et peccatum, dummodo sit eorum quae quis scire tenetur et potest. Et ideo talis ignorantia non totaliter excusat a peccato. Si vero sit talis ignorantia quae **omnino** sit involuntaria, sive quia est invincibilis, sive quia est eius quod quis scire non tenetur; talis ignorantia omnino excusat a peccato.—*ibid.*, a.3, c.; Trans.: *ibid.*, 932.

64. See *Summa Theologica, ibid.* a.2, c., 53.

65. Ex quo patet quod nulla ignorantia invincibilis est peccatum.—*ibid.*

66. Ignorantia vincibilis est peccatum, si sit eorum quae aliquis scire tenetur; non autem si sit eorum quae quis scire non tenetur.—*loc. cit.*

67. See Regatillo-Zalba, *Summa,* 104 ff.; Prümmer, *Manuale,* 34, ff.; Merkelbach, *Summa,* 80ff.

68. Ignorantia iuris non excusat, quia ipsa peccatum est; sed ignorantia facti excusat. *In II Sent.,* d. 21, q. 2, a. 2, ad 4, 595.

69. Ignorantia iuris non excusat a peccato, nisi forte sit ignorantia invincibilis, . . . quae omnino excusat.—*Quodl.* 3, q. 12, a. 27, ad 2, 427.

70. Ignoranta . . . quae rationem culpae habet excusat quidem quantum ad aliquid, scilicet, in quantum ignorantia est, quia sic habet quod involuntarium causat; non autem excusat in quantum culpa est, quia sic rationem voluntarii retinet; et ideo ignorantia universalis excusat peccatum sequens non toto sed a tanto.—*In II Sent.,* d. 22, q. 2, a. 2, sol., 293.

71. Aliquis de hoc quod non confiteur peccata quae nescit esse peccata propter ignorantiam iuris divini, non excusatur a fictione.—*In IV Sent.,* d. 21, q. 2, a. 2, 595.

72. See *Quodl.* 1, q. 9, a. 19, 374-5.

73. Bertke, *The Possibility of Invincible Ignorance*, 56-7.

74. See *Summa Theologica*, I-II, q. 19, a. 6, c., 146-7; Lottin, *Psychologie et morale*, 405-6.

75. See above, pp. 75-9.

76. See De Blic, J., "Probabilisme," *Dictionnaire de la foi catholique* 4 (1922) 306-12; Lottin, "Le tutiorisme du XIIIe siècle," *RTAM* 5 (1933) 299-300.

77. See *De Veritate*, q. 17, a. 4, resp., 77.

78. Verba autem illa D. Thomae: 'Quod agitur contra legem . . . ' intelligenda esse cum hac exceptione: Nisi conscientia erret invincibiliter et inculpabiliter. . . . Et iure quidem: constans enim est D. Thomae sententia, conscientiam invincibiliter erroneam a peccato excusare.—Deman, Th., O. P., "Eclairissements sur quodlibet VIII, a. 13," *DT* 38 (1935) 53-60. Quotation is found on p. 60.

79. See above, p. 79 and fn. 46.

80. See Frins, *De Actibus Humanis*, 110, ff.

81. Ex conscientia autem obligatur aliquis ad peccatum, sive habeat certam fidem de contrario eius quod agit, sive etiam habeat opinionem cum aliqua dubitatione. Illud autem quod agitur contra legem semper est malum, nec excusatur per hoc quod est secundum conscientiam.—*Quodl.* 8, q. 6, a. 13, 540.

82. See p. 33.

83. See *De Veritate*, q. 17, a. 5, resp., 79.

84. See *ibid.*, ad 1.

85. See St. Bonaventure, *In II Sent.*, d. 39, a. 1.

86. Because the word *especially* is used, it may be that Bonaventure also is including indifferent acts commanded by the superior, which will be treated below, and evil acts. In the latter case, the subject's conscience would be a true one, and Bonaventure would not be in agreement with Thomas.

87. See above, p. 31.

88. Si fiat aliquid quod est secundum se malum, quod errans ratio judicat bonum, peccatum non evitatur; si autem non fiat, peccatum incurritur.—*In II Sent.*, d. 39, q. 3, a. 3, sol., 525.

89. See *loc. cit.* and ad 5.
90. See Lottin, *Psychologie et morale*, 389-90.
91. See Lottin, "La valeur normative de la conscience morale," *ETL* 9 (1932) 429.
92. See *ibid.*, 431.
93. See *De Veritate*, q. 17, a. 4, resp.
94. See Lottin, *Psychologie*, 397.
95. Utrum voluntas concordans rationi erranti sit bona? — *Summa Theologica*, I-II, q. 19, a. 6.
96. Utrum voluntas discordans rationi erranti sit mala?
97. See Lottin, "Les éléments de la moralité des acts chez S. Thomas d'aquin," *RNScP* 24 (1922) 418-26.
98. Quand il s'agit des circonstances d'un fait, à supposer même qu'on puisse les connaître, d'ordinaire on ne doit pas s'en enquérir; l'ignorance ou l'on se trouve à leur sujet (ignorantia facti) n'est nullement coupable; l'acte subséquent n'est donc entaché d'aucune faute morale. Mais il faudra raisonner tout autrement, si l'ignorance porte sur la malice morale objective d'un acte (ignorantia iuris). Sans doute il arrive qu'on puisse connaître cette dernière; saint Thomas a prévu ces cas d'impossibilité ou d'ignorance invincible: manifestement ils excusent de toute faute. Mais à supposer que l'on puisse avoir cette connaissance de l'ordre objectif, on doit l'acquérir: ici, qui peut, doit. Et même une advertance actuelle à cette obligation de vaincre l'ignorance ne serait pas requise, pour rendre cette ignorance coupable; l'advertance, que les anciens appelaient interprétative, suffirait ici pour endendrer le désordre moral, nous ne disons pas le désordre complet que comporte une faute grave, mais ce désordre imparfait que saint Thomas appelle faute légère.

Nous sommes dès lors, en état de répondre à cette dernière instance que l'on pourra faire. Puisque d'après saint Thomas, il n'y a pas d'actes individuels indifférents, du fait qu'un acte mauvaise en soi apparaît erronément comme moralement bon, saint Thomas ne peut se contenter de l'exempter de faute, il doit le proclamer formellement bon. S. Thomas répond sans ambages en cet article sixième: L'erreur de conscience peut provenir d'une ignorance de principe portant sur la malice objective de l'acte considéré *in abstracto;* dans ce cas, l'acte résultant de cette erreur, loin d'être formellement bon, est formellement mauvais, parce que, hormis le

cas d'une impossibilité physique de s'enquérir de la loi morale, cet
acte procède d'une ignorance conséquente, volontaire, de ce que l'on
devrait savior. Il importe peu à cet égard que cet acte soit rapporté à une fin bonne; comme on le dira à l'article suivant, la
poursuite d'une fin louable ne suffit pas pour rendre bon un acte
mauvais; l'acte de celui qui veut mentir pour sauver son ami est
et rest mauvais malgré la noblesse de but poursuivi. Mais un
second cas peut se présenter: l'erreur vient d'une ignorance de
détail, portant sur des circonstances de l'acte concret que l'on ne
pouvait ou que l'on ne devait pas connaître; alors l'acte résultant
de cette erreur ne peut être ni bon ni mauvais. Cet acte procède
en effet d'une ignorance antécédente, involontaire, de ce qu'on
ne devait pas connaître; or, l'erreur antécédente enlève tout car-
actere de volontaire et dès lors toute moralité formelle à l'acte qui
en émane. . . . C'est en vain qu'on voudrait acculer s. Thomas à se
prononcer sur la moralité d'un tel acte. Le s. Docteur à bon droit
se réfuse. C'est au sujet des seuls actes délibérés qu'il a déclaré
impossible leur indifférence morale. Or, l'acte en tant qu'il procède d'une ignorance antécédente de fait n'est pas délibéré au
point de vue moral, ni en soi comme il est manifeste, ni dans sa
cause, puisque l'erreur est involontaire et innocente. Sans doute,
cet acte concret pourra être rapporté à une fin et par la même il
sera délibéré; et il faut ajouter qui si cette fin est bonne, rien ici
n'empêche que la bonté de la fin ne pénètre l'acte lui-même,
puisque, l'acte n'étant pas mauvais, rien de la part de celui-ci ne
fait obstacle à cette inpregnation. L'acte sera bon, parce qu'il aura
été ultérieurement orienté vers une fin moralement bonne; mais
cet acte en tant qu'il procède d'une ignorance antécédente, n'est ni
bon ni mauvais; il est étranger à l'ordre de la moralité formelle,
puis qu'un élément éssentiel de celle-ci, la délibération, lui fait
défaut.—*ibid.*, 427-9.

99. See Frins, *op. cit.*, 127.

100. Non dantur opera indifferentia in individuo quae ex deliberata
ratione manant; sunt vero indifferentia quae ex necessitate pro-
ficiscuntur. Concina, D., O. P., *Theologia Christiana—Compendium*
1 (Bononiae, 1766) 35.

101. Proclamat etiam esse intolerabilem absurditatem, quod quis ex
scelere, e.gr., ex idolatria, cum ignorantia invincibili commissa,
mereatur vitam aeternam. Sic ille: 'Quidnam communi sensui
repugnantius quam scelera et horrenda flagitia portentosa meta-
morphosi in virtutes, in meritum vitae aeternae transformari? Qua
vi? Divina? Absit. Qua ergo? Audi et obstupesce: vi erroris hu-
mani. Error igitur mentis nostrae est alter Deus.'—Concina, *De
Conscientia*, lib. 1, c.5, quoted by Prümmer, *op. cit.*, 205.

102. See Prümmer, *loc. cit.;* Regatillo-Zalba, *Summa,* 258-9.

103. See LaCroix, C., S. J., *Theologia Moralis* 1 (Ravenna, 1756) lib. 1, tr. 1, 82b.

104. See Sertillanges, A. D., O. P., *La philosophie morale de s. Thomas d'aquin* (Aubier, ed. Montaigne, Paris, 1946) 388-9.

105. See *ibid.,* 390.

106. See *ibid.,* 392-4.

107. Le bien en soi est une règle en soi. Le bien selon nous (la volonté étant supposée droite) est une règle pours nous. Il ne faut pas croiser, et déclarer qu'un bien en soi se trouve par cela seul, *hic et nunc,* notre règle; ni davantage qu'un bien selon nous en devienne bien en soi. Quand je vise au bien tel qu'il m'apparaît, je suis, *en tant qu'un agent volontaire,* qualifié par le bien, quoique l'objectivité du cas puisse être autre. Même n'ayant pas suivi *la* loi, j'ai pu suîvre ma loi, et, comme sujet moral, être en règle. Parler ainsi, ce n'est pas rendre la morale subjective; mais seulement la moralité du sujet, ce qui est tout naturel.—*ibid.,* 396.

108. See above, pp. 93, ff.

109. See *Summa Theologica,* I-II, q. 19, a. 6.

110. See *Quodl.* 3, a. 27; *Summa Theologica,* Suppl., q. 49, a.4.

111. See *Summa Theologica* I-II, q. 19, a. 5, resp.

112. See Frins, *op. cit.,* 127-32; Prümmer, *op. cit.,* 205, footnote 44.

113. See also Regatillo-Zalba, *op. cit.,* 258-9; Aertnys-Damen, *op. cit.,* 71; Bouquillon, *Theologia Moralis,* 491.

114. Cum actus recipiat speciem ab obiecto, non recipit speciem ab eo secundum materiam objecti, sed secundum rationem objecti. . . . Omnis autem actus humanus habet rationem peccati vel meriti, in quantum est voluntarius: obiectum autem voluntatis est bonum prout apprehensum: et ideo actus humanus iudicatur virtuosus vel vitiosus secundum bonum apprehensum in quod per se voluntas fertur, et non secundum materiale obiectum actus.—*Quodl.* 3, a. 27. See also *S. Th.,* I-II, q. 19, a. 5.

We have seen that the representative writings of the Franciscan School of the thirteenth century taught that conscience is a habit, imposing an obligation which is based on the intrinsic morality of the act dictated. The Franciscans of the time were preoccupied with the role of objective morality, to the detriment of the subjective order. If the act dictated by conscience is good, one must obey the conscience. If the act is objectively evil, the conscience must be set aside. If the act is indifferent, one must either obey the conscience, for an indifferent act receives its morality from the dictate of conscience, or one can set aside the conscience without sin. If one obeys the dictate of conscience and performs an evil act, the act is and remains evil; no merit is possible. This School did not seem to admit the excuse of ignorance.

In Saint Albert, the beginning of a new concept is seen. Conscience is defined as an act, the conclusion of a syllogism. As long as one is subjectively convinced that this judgment is dictating something right, one must obey the conscience.

Saint Thomas expanded the teachings of Saint Albert. For Aquinas, the moral conscience is an act, a syllogistic judgment of the practical reason, dictating the morality of an act about to be performed. It imposes an obligation if it prescribes or forbids, for it is through conscience that man comes to a knowledge of the law as applied to a particular action. If the conscience happens to be erroneous, it obliges as long as its dictate endures. If the error is invincible and the cause of a subsequent act, that act is involuntary, and therefore inculpable. If the error is here and now vincible, i.e., one can here and now overcome the error and also has an obligation to do so, he must rectify his conscience. If he nevertheless acts according to the dictate of such a conscience, he sins; likewise sin is committed if he does not obey the conscience while it endures. If the conscience is erroneous because of vincible and culpable ignorance which cannot now be overcome because one does not advert to that fact, the act is sinful in its cause, but here and now it is not formally sinful.

It is our opinion that it is the implicit teaching of Saint Thomas that one can gain merit by following an invincibly erroneous conscience, since it is the formal object which specifies an act. In the case of an act prescribed by an invincibly erroneous conscience, i.e., here and now invincible, it is the good as apprehended, not the good *in se,* which is the formal object. Therefore, it is this good as apprehended which specifies the act. The act is morally good, and if the other conditions required for merit are present, the act is also meritorious.

By pointing out in the discussion of the Franciscan position their preoccupation with the problem of objective morality and the solution proposed by the Dominicans, the balance between the objective and subjective orders of morality was indicated. Conscience, the subjective norm, obliges only because it is the application of the objective norm, the eternal law. If conscience does not represent the objective norm in fact, it either represents what is honestly believed to be that norm, or its error is vincible and culpable. In the former case, it is normative *per accidens;* in the latter case, one must overcome the error by the use of moral diligence or through study, and thus render the conscience conformable to the eternal law.

Thus, the objective norm of morality has a prime place as a determinant of moral conduct. It is not simply a guidepost, as those who teach situation ethics would hold. It is the moral law, with absolute values, which must be obeyed. God is interested in conformity to this law, and not only in a right intention. Were the intention sufficient, the conclusion that an end justifies the means would be inevitable. Christian morality would become chaotic; one could justify any action with his intention, with no regard for the law of God.

This has been the constant teaching of theologians. From the present study it is abundantly clear that even in the thirteenth century both the supremacy of the objective moral order and the legitimate role of erroneous conscience as an accidental norm of morality were acknowledged. But there is no place in this theology for the morality of situation ethics. An ,essentially subjective and relativistic criterion cannot supplant the law given us by God. "Heaven and earth shall pass away, but my word shall not pass away." (*Matt.* 24:35)

BIOGRAPHICAL NOTE

XAVIER GILBERT COLAVECHIO was born in Philadelphia, Pennsylvania, April 7, 1931. He attended St. Gabriel Parochial School, and was graduated from Southeast Catholic High School, Philadelphia in June, 1948. He entered the Norbertine Order at St. Norbert Abbey, August 28, 1948. He received his degree of Bachelor of Arts in Philosophy from St. Norbert College in June, 1952. In September, 1953, he began his studies at the Gregorian University, Rome, from which he received the degree of Licentiate in Sacred Theology in July, 1957. He was ordained in LaStorta, Italy, on June 29, 1955.